Why the Green New Deal is Good for America

by Christopher Kinkaid

I0415480

Drawings
by
Toby Kinkaid

ISBN: 9781091826915

Table of Contents

About the Author

Christopher (Toby) Kinkaid

Christopher (Toby) Kinkaid, from Portland, Oregon, has worked in the clean energy field for over three decades. Mr. Kinkaid is the inventor of the patented "**Helyx**" Vertical Axis Wind Generator, the "**Mariposa**" Non-imaging solar concentrator PV module (continuous operation at Sandia National Laboratory since 1994), the **Solar Demultiplexer** optical solar concentrating lens (Dr. James/Sandia National Laboratory 1991), and the original "**Solar Power Pack**" (Mother Earth News, "**Littlest Utility**" June/July, 2001). Mr. Kinkaid has been an official lecturer and presenter on clean energy technology around the world including "APEC", Bangkok, Thailand, 2003, "Energy Solutions World", Tokyo, Japan, 2003, the International Biomass Conference (IBC), 2010, Minneapolis, MN, and the Algal Biomass Organization (ABO) Conference, 2010, Phoenix, AZ.

Mr. Kinkaid has appeared in TV interviews on KOIN TV, KGW TV, FOX 12 NEWS and "Sustainable Today" produced in Oregon.

Mr. Kinkaid has served on the board of directors for the National Hydrogen Association, in Washington D.C., 1993, and the Japanese Satellite Communications Company (JCNET), Fukuoka, Japan, 1994, Oregon Wind Corporation 2003-2007, and Algaedyne Corporation (2008-2011).

Christopher (Toby) Kinkaid is based in Portland, Oregon, and continues his work in clean energy technology, intellectual property, and applications.

Preface

"Is the Green New Deal the new Socialism? ... Do they really want to take away our piston engines?"

- Chris Wallace - Fox News Sunday - (2019)

The Green New Deal is based on facts, not fears.

The facts involve the toxic footprint of our global addiction to Fossil Fuel energy, and its destruction of biology worldwide.

The Green New Deal is about creating new wealth directly where it is needed most, solving global problems with local solutions starting with solar powered solutions for electricity, heating/cooling, and transportation fuels all produced onsite where they're used.

One hundred years ago, Chris Wallace might well have asked "Do they want to take away our horse and buggies!"

Industrial revolution always has its detractors along the way satisfied with a business as usual world, and un-eager to change the status quo. However, the toxicity of fossil fuels have polluted and choked our natural systems to such extent industrial evolution becomes our only path forward.

Climate disruption, global toxicity and the collapse of species, with energy only available as a commodity, are all caused by doing one thing: burning carbon.

The Green New Deal recognizes the connection of energy, environment and economy and how all the toxic man made global catastrophes we face can be solved by doing one thing: evolve out of burning carbon fuels and into clean fuels.

Fossil fuels powered the 18th, 19th and 20th centuries, respectively, but the needs of the 21st century are just not met with an 18th century approach.

The Green New Deal is about the industrial revolution of the 21st century - the obsolescence of Carbon fuels and the liberation of a new era of energy abundance and security based on industrial solar fuels. The Green New Deal is about Capitalism, not socialism

Fossil fuels dominate our modern world supplying over 80% of the energy we currently use causing a toxic collapse. Such dependence on burning carbon has left us an accumulating toxicity across the globe, climate disruption, loss of species, deforestation, loss of habitat and ecosystems, high energy costs, social inequities, and baked-in income disparity worldwide.

Fossil fuels have left us with Climate Disruption and a death spiral measured by the increased toxic corruption of our soils, air, water and biology worldwide.

Opposition to the Green New Deal often use misdirection and disinformation to continue the deception of "fossil fuels are necessary for a modern lifestyle." Name calling such as "socialism", and "they want to take your piston engines away" reveal a Luddite mentality unaware of the history unfolding around them.

The new clean energy economy is all about capitalism, not socialism. Open up the energy markets to locally produced clean electricity and fuels, and capitalism will flourish. Empower the individual, and capitalism thrives with new products, services, and economy: given access to energy.

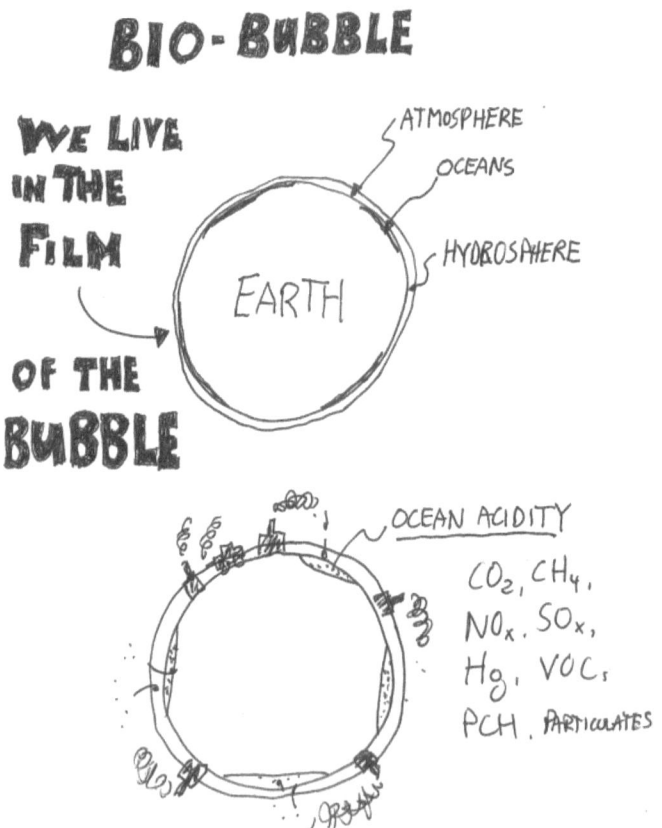

Consider the question, is CO2 a pollutant? The fossil fuel industry claims CO2 is not a pollutant.

Disregarding the definition of pollution as "anything deleterious to a system," the opposition to industrial evolution again tries misdirection by ignoring the basic meaning of words. Anything can be a pollution, if in excess. Including CO_2.

Billions of years ago when early life was developing, Oxygen could be considered the first pollutant as photosynthesis ejected Oxygen as a waste product. Anything in excess can be a pollution. We're made mostly of water, yet too much water and we drown. If the pH of our blood is too acidic or too alkaline our cells cease to function. Too much Mercury in our system and our organs fail. All biology, including the earth, has sweet-spots where everything works the best.

Outside of certain ranges life for any species is extremely fragile. Pollution, is anything in excess of a system's ability to tolerate.

"Dose makes the poison"

-Ancient medical wisdom-

Too much CO_2 in our environment is indeed a pollutant as millions of tons of daily emissions worldwide cause large amounts of Carbonic acid to be formed when CO_2 and water mix. Acid rain from CO_2, Nitrous Oxides (NOx), and Sulfurous Oxides (SOx) emissions distributed all over the planet result in the acidification of our ponds, lakes, streams, rivers and oceans causing catastrophic stress on species around the globe.

Our blood pH is very close to seawater. Even slight variants of our blood pH can be catastrophic for a human being. The same principles are in play with aquatic life on all levels.

Keep loading the atmosphere and oceans with CO_2 and acidity will disrupt the base of the food web collapsing the ocean ecosystem.

Too much CO_2 emitted in our hydrosphere traps heat on a global scale raising the temperature of the atmosphere and ocean surfaces due to the Green House effect fueling thermodynamically larger and larger climatic events (hurricanes, typhoons, tornados) costing human lives, loss of livestock and wildlife, species displacement, and property damage costing billions of dollars per major event.

Too much new CO_2 rapidly warming the arctic drops the temperature difference between the poles and the equator destabilizing the stratosphere Jet Stream introducing a new global danger capable of killing people, livestock, and wildlife per event: the Polar Vortex.

In 2018, the polar vortex dropped an air mass measuring 50 degrees below zero F temperatures in the upper midwest. There is a direct link between increasing temperatures in the arctic due to massive CO_2 influx and the Polar Vortex.

Too much CO_2 in the atmosphere drives up temperatures which unabated will increase the thaw rate of the tundra and permafrost releasing massive amounts of methane, an extreme greenhouse gas, which only exacerbates further warming.

Increased warming of the seas threaten the destruction of coral reefs and all specialized ecosystems in our soils, air, water and biology. It all builds up with an inertia we can no longer ignore.

Too much of anything can be a pollutant. Too much CO_2 in our environment due to spewing out millions of tons per day of carbon previously sequester is a global disaster.

The ancient Greeks long expressed a principle in their philosophy for health: "nothing in excess."

The Green New Deal is about the industrial revolution of the 21st century, the transition from Carbon fuel dependency, to non-carbon fuel independence and the economic opportunity this unleashes in the American and global economy.

The Green New Deal is good for America because it addresses each major problem facing our world, our country, and each citizen by recognizing the relationship between energy, economy, prosperity, and the global and local environment vital to us all - are all tied into energy potency and supply.

Pollution anywhere becomes pollution everywhere with the winds and tides. Fukushima is still spewing radiation into the Pacific with impacts across the oceans showing up on the west coast of America. We're all connected by the world we share.

The Green New Deal is good for America as it recognizes and embraces a real solution for a sustainable and prosperous economy founded on universal access to clean energy using 21st century technology. Get energy right and everything works. Get energy wrong, and nothing can work at all.

Given the toxic trends of our addiction to a fossil fuel powered world, our entire future depends on what we do, or fail to do, over the next decade. How we exit the decade of the 2020s will set the course for the rest of the century. Our choice is whether our industrial direction is moving forward with more energy, more access and non-toxicity for a sustainable and growing future, or a continued spiral down into toxic collapse.

Collapse of our fisheries, forests, farmlands, wetlands, fields, waterways, soils, air, oceans, and biology from the accumulated toxicity of fossil fuels is inevitable - if we continue a Carbon fueled world. Modern civilization, as any organism when greatly stressed, either adapts, or dies.

Three centuries of fossil fuel use and a maturing clean energy technology have converged in the 21st century and will determine our collective fate as a civilization.

The industrial revolution of the new clean energy economy will obsolete the fossil fuel energy paradigm, which has ruled industrial civilization for three hundred years, and replace it with an entirely new paradigm. A paradigm of non-Carbon fuels, non-toxic, distributed, and with no fuel costs, as renewable energy is captured, stored and dispatched on demand creating a new source of distributed wealth.

There is an industrial revolution emerging in the 21st century, and it starts as an energy revolution. A revolution from unsustainable global toxicity, to sustainability and economic growth for the next century. A revolution from poverty and toxicity, into self-reliance, and prosperity. A revolution from fuel costs for everyone, to no fuel costs for anyone.

The Green New Deal is about the industrial revolution of the 21st century: sustainability.

Dominated by fossil fuels, at last modern civilization has the tools and technology to evolve out of Carbon fuels (the source of most worldwide toxicity), and into a sustainable, non-toxic energy paradigm producing new wealth for America, and all other countries by opening up a new source of power: the industrial sun.

As other countries move from poverty to middle class, they become consumers. Consumers become markets. And markets, are good for America worldwide so we can meet this new demand with our own economic growth.

A Green New Deal is good for America, as it reduces local pollution and health impacts from the energy industry on industrial scale lowering real costs for Americans, and increases the power density of fuels to increase freedom, the machines we wish to use, and unleash a new age of distributed power supply offering everyone, everywhere more options for electronics, communications, manufacturing, and transportation. All with no fuel costs, or toxicity.

A Green New Deal is the greatest economic opportunity in the history of industrialization because it's based on generating distributed hard currency derived from a known resource already distributed throughout the world: solar electricity.

Based on solar electric photovoltaics (PV) modules, and the chemistry of water, a new economy will emerge unleashing our modern civilization from the limits, toxicity, and abuses of fossil fuels controlled by a few, into a paradigm where mass market consumers can produce all the energy they need to power their technology onsite, with no fuel costs or toxicity.

This new solar powered wealth increases individual freedom and productivity in a practical manner, starting with lower energy costs for immediate payback. Solar costs are intrinsically lower than a fossil fuel costs as there are no fuel cost components, and therefore no toxicity liabilities.

The new economy isn't based on just the consumption of energy, as it has for three centuries, it's based on the local production of energy consumed on the spot, or stored for later use directly by the consumer. A new energy independence.

The classic notions of economy as Supply and Demand as applied to the energy industry is put on its head with the advent of distributed resources (DR). Before, if you, (the Demand), needed energy you had to buy it from someone (Supply). In the new economy, those lines blur. With the right technology, you don't need to pay for a "supply" of energy, you make it yourself, all you pay for is hardware and maintenance, there is no fuel cost.

Under the solar paradigm most or all of the energy needed by a consumer can be produced onsite, where you use it. Energy doesn't need to be transported when using solar.

If you have the technology, you have the sun. If you have the sun, then you can get it done. Any individual, residential, commercial, or industrial load can be solar powered.

The phase out of fossil fuels follows the historical trend of all technologies developed in the 1800s, in our century there's a better way. Just as Kodak, and Polaroid were founded in the 1800s and eventually became outdated and collapsed, so the fossil fuel world and piston engines at last will find their end, to be replaced with the next generation of engine technology: the fuel cell.

The new energy paradigm of a Green New Deal is based on generating new wealth. A source of wealth accessible by all people with the right technology. Since the sun falls everywhere on earth, distributed new wealth turns solar generated electricity directly into hard currency.

Solar PV panels produce electricity, and electricity is a hard currency. Worth American dollars, Yen, Pounds, Euros, and any other currency. Electricity is currency, if you can produce it. With solar PV anyone can produce clean energy, and with the proper battery technology (hydrogen fuel from water), have a self-reliant, sustainable and resilient energy supply.

What happens when the sun doesn't shine? Energy storage technology. A new energy paradigm is described which doesn't just solve America's energy problem with toxicity and high costs, but goes further to point out we have a global problem with toxicity and fuel costs, and we need a global solution which works on a local level.

Local and global solutions in the same hardware package.

The issues center around the impacts an excess of CO_2 presents. In excess, too much CO_2 is clearly a pollutant on all fronts.

The pH of the oceans is falling (becoming more acidic). Disrupt the basic chemistry of the base of the food web, and the consequences are dire for present and future generations.

It gets worse. Toxins accumulate in biological systems (including you and me, and every other species). As more and more toxins are released by our fossil fuel use more impacts would be expected. How much is too much?

We're well past that point. We started to tip the environment in the 1970s to which Earth Day was a response. Global toxicity was even then destroying ecosystems from wetlands, forests, farmland, and fields. Deforestation was consuming the Amazon already at alarming rates back in the 1970s.

The next decade of the 2020s will prove to be the most important in modern human history. Do we make the path forward beneficial for everyone? Or, do we continue our spiral into toxic collapse.

Our energy paradigm will define the path.

The Green New Deal recognizes the best path is toward empowering individuals everywhere with a modern industrial power supply which doesn't charge for fuel. This path is the foundation and the very means of production the Green New Deal unleashes.

There is a new world order, and it's no longer based on Carbon. It's based on sunlight and water.

About the Book

This book examines the specifics of why a Green New Deal is good for America. Through this book we'll examine the role of energy in civilization historically, and how Industrial Revolution always brings economic and social advancement.

Since the industrial age three hundred years ago energy has been dominated by fossil fuels.

A Green New Deal challenges this old paradigm replacing fossil fuels with a more powerful, safer, more available and non-toxic energy system.

A clean energy economy which simultaneously address issues from lowering toxicity to dynamic job creation across all sectors of our economy and eliminates the toxicity of fossil fuels.

The toxicity and impacts of using Carbon-based fuels for three centuries have thrust our modern civilization into a death spiral as toxicity chokes modern biological systems, which if continued will result in increased Climate Disruption, Chemical and Biological Disruption, and an eventual collapse of modern civilization, following the path of every other civilization known in history.

This book examines the problems produced when energy is based on Carbon fuels, and what Science offers to provide an evolution in our energy paradigm away from toxicity and centralized control, into renewable energy already distributed operating with no fuel costs, or toxicity.

At the time of this writing over 7 billion people live on planet earth. A Green New Deal described in this book outlines from a thermodynamic perspective why a new energy paradigm is required in the 21st century.

In this book we'll examine the historic march of fuels through the centuries and how increased specific energy density in fuels, and the engines to use them, unleashes industrial and social revolution in step.

The Green New Deal offers a real solution for local and global toxicity releasing a new industrial revolution in the 21st century: sustainability on industrial scale.

Introduction

"It is far from easy to determine whether she (Nature) has proved to man a kind parent, or a merciless stepmother."

- Pliny the Elder, Natural History

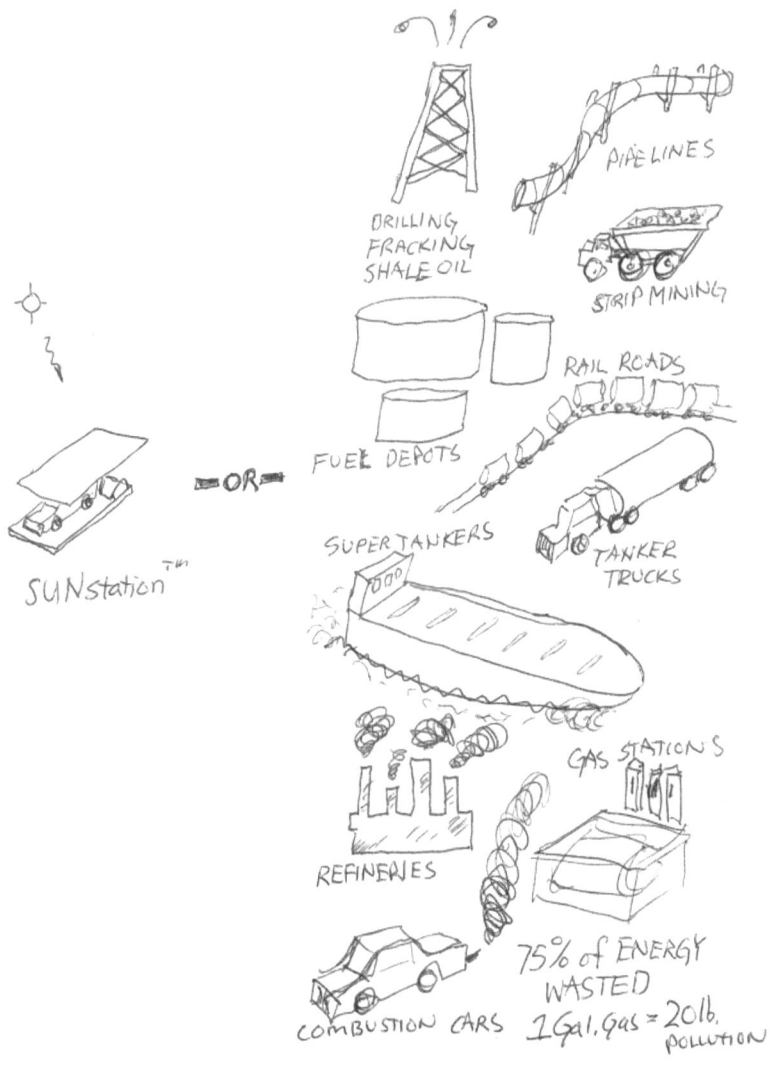

The world economy runs on energy. Manufacturing, Communications, Electronics and Transportation all depend on industrial amounts of energy both electrical and chemical.

Since the industrial age world economies have grown at enormous rates, on the backs of consuming vast amounts of carbon fuels. Half of all the toxins released into the environment over human history have appeared in the last 30 years reflecting our gigantic and ever growing appetite for resources, and our willingness to "discharge" our toxins into the environment at ever increasing rates - to our great peril.

The problem with dumping toxins in soils, water ways, the atmosphere and oceans, forcing its exposure to biological systems, are the impacts of toxic Bioaccumulation.

Bioaccumulation is another toxic time bomb as more and more toxins are absorbed into the flesh and organs of fish and animals throughout the food web upon which we all depend. The higher the organism the more prone to toxins accumulating in the body, this danger includes human beings. Eat tainted food, and you can become ill.

Continue business as usual and we condemn the earth to suffer a continued rise in global toxicity with increased Climate Disruption, to endure ever increasing climatic calamity costing billions per event, or, we can choose a new path. A leap forward, not backward in the energy evolutionary tree.

The world environment is in collapse, and a continued use of highly toxic fossil fuels and the economic inequity implicit when energy, needed by all, is controlled and parceled out by a few has reached its logical conclusion: un-sustainability. The only answer is to industrially evolve.

Our world holds over 7 billion souls. Each human being needing clean air, water, soils, food, waste treatment, and energy in both electricity and chemical fuels.

Thermodynamically, to bring everyone above the poverty level will require an industrial fuel and energy paradigm which moves us forward, not backward.

We need an energy paradigm which provides a real means of obsoleting poverty, the only way it could be done - when primary energy is accessible by all where they are.

Under the fossil fuel world view for over three centuries, the world suffers a toxic runaway train with accumulating toxins threatening to collapse species and ecosystems worldwide, including ourselves if we don't act.

History will know the decade of the 2020s as the tipping point. Everything depends on what we do, or fail to do in this decade. It's important we get energy right.

Everything important is at stake in the very survivability of a stressed earth assailed on all fronts by our generation's complacency with trashing our fragile earth. For 7 billion people to survive, and indeed prosper a new paradigm of energy is required which must be energy potent.

The industrial revolution of the 21st century will break the bonds of fossil fuels, the epitome of "have" and "have-not" by applying the technology we have to package solar technology, battery and power conditioning available onsite, not energy delivered to the load as with fossil fuels.

The Green New Deal seeks the creation of a world of "haves" and "haves" by providing a distributed form of new wealth creation: sunlight into electrons doing work into hard currency.

Solar technology, provides the primary power supply for our individual, residential, commercial and industrial needs. A power supply which provides real wealth to all people who wish to tap into the ultimate power supply, the power supply which runs the entire natural world, and soon our industrial: the sun.

Ending poverty worldwide is not some insurmountable problem, which only a utopian dream can entertain. It's as straight forward as having the right technology, and sizing the solar power supply to the load.

Tap into the sun, produce electricity, store it, and release it formatted to what ever load you're powering. That's it. Not so difficult really. All one really needs is the right gear.

In the 21st century fossil fuels have become obsolete. We've outgrown Carbon based fuels. You can still power an engine with petroleum distillates, but why would you want to?

They're inefficient, toxic when used, and as a commodity, fuel needs to be purchased again as soon as they're used, locking the consumer into an "industrial drug" which always must be repurchased, in short, Carbon fuels are expensive.

Further, when we use fossil fuels we waste 75% of the energy out the tailpipe spewing toxins which linger and harm the environment for centuries.

Is this the energy system the opponents are defending?

We go to all the effort, cost and environmental damage to extract fossil fuels, only to use them and waste 75% of the energy out the exhaust spewing toxins. How does this make sense for a 21st century world?

In broad strokes doesn't sound good at all. The simple fact is we don't need Carbon for industrial energy at all. And it's time to make the jump.

A Green New Deal recognizes this moment in history.

$$\phi + \bigcirc = \$$$

SUNLIGHT + WATER = HARD CURRENCY

The equation, on the front cover, sums up the new energy paradigm of the age. A formula for peace. How the production of clean electricity and clean fuels is a path to industrial freedom for all economies.

Solar energy plus Water equals Hard Currency. The essential formula upon which world peace in the 21st century can include everyone, everywhere.

This relationship is the key to economic prosperity for all countries with a distributed power supply for growth far into the future.

America has an interest in seeing the world stabilize. America has an interest in leading the way. It is our nature when unleashed.

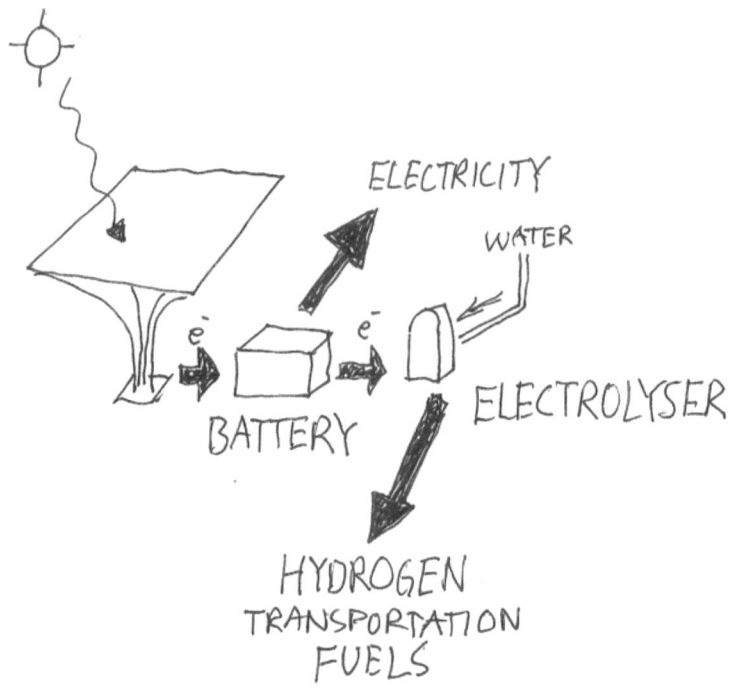

Power plants in the 21st century

Sunlight with photovoltaics (PV) produces primary electricity. Add electricity to water (through an electrolyser) produces clean high power hydrogen fuel (storing energy, and available to fuel all heavy trucks, construction, farm equipment, buildings, charging stations and power plants). Using a fuel cell engine hydrogen, and oxygen from the air are recombined back into water releasing most of the energy.

A water cycle, where water is used, disassociated into gases, stored as energy, and recombined back into water releasing most of the energy. Water is stable, and entirely non-toxic.

This is the basis of the water cycle.

The world is mostly covered with water, the human body is mostly made of water, and water is the result of the most powerful fuel oxidation we know. Amazing. Use hydrogen fuel, and our industrial waste product is pure water. Use water as a feedstock, add renewable energy and produce clean, powerful hydrogen fuel. The water cycle.

No Carbon needed. No Carbon involved. There are no more Green House Gas (GHG) emissions, no NOx, no SOx, no particulates, no Volatile Organic Compounds (VOC), or Partially Consumed Hydrocarbons (PCH), or continued Mercury poisoning. All of these problems are based on, and caused by burning Carbon. The answer? Let's stop burning carbon, and jump into the 21st century using fuel cells, as we used back in the 1960s on Apollo.

NASA chose Fuel Cells as the primary production of electricity on Apollo for good reasons. Hydrogen fuel cells were the only fuel and oxidant known to produce water, vital for the lives of the astronauts. Hydrogen and Oxygen recombined through a fuel cell were the only technology "compatible" with human life. All other schemes were toxic and therefore overly dangerous for space flight. If it works for NASA, why not the rest of us?

No continued acidification of the oceans and waterways. A clean energy economy doesn't just address and solve our energy problem. A Green New Deal address all of our problems. All of these toxins are no longer required.

Solve everyone's energy problem, and we can eliminate 17 additional global problems. As an industrial civilization our problems are global. The answer combines the local with the global by solving both groups of problems with one common solution: leave Carbon fuels behind. Evolve into the "Silicon Man."

The best kept industrial secret is "you don't need Carbon."
The energy in fossil fuels has essentially nothing to do with the
Carbon. The energy is, and has always been, in the hydrogen
stuck to the Carbon.

The Green New Deal recognizes that fossil fuels are really an
18th century technology trying to fill a 21st century need.

Just as we don't use old clicking telegraphs to send and
receive messages over a wire, we use our modern smart
phones. Our daily communications using smart phones
represents a trillion times more capability than the old
telegraphs.

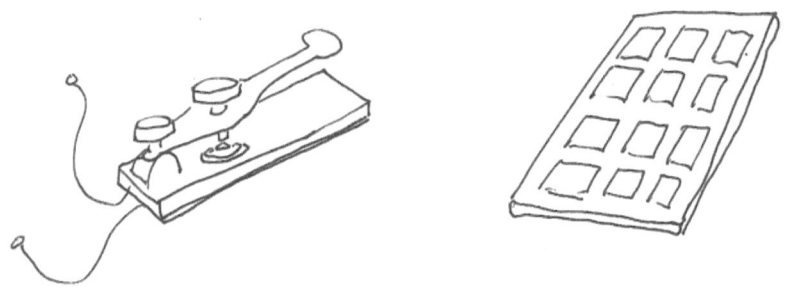

We use smart phones because they're better than the
telegraphs from the 1850s, because we live in the 21st
century. The same is true today with energy. Why use
petroleum distillates and piston engines as we did in 1880 for
a world with 21st century populations and needs? Just as we
don't use telegraphs, we soon won't use pistons.

This is the natural evolution of industrial revolution.

We don't live in the communications world of the 18th century
anymore. The time has come for fossil fuels, a paradigm
started in the 17th century, to follow suit. The industrial 21st

century will use sunlight and water for primary energy, storage and conversion and have more power, more choices, no toxicity, unlimited access and use for all countries. This is the formula for peace. Real peace is founded on real freedom.

What could be more American?

The world is upon an industrial revolution. A revolution of leashing human potential, creativity, and individual freedom, as the American revolution and the rise of the 1st Industrial revolution expanded human potential. The liberation of economic stimulus all over the world will be felt as our civilization takes the industrial jump beyond fossil fuels and all of the toxicity and inequity it enslaves, to a new era of clean energy, empowering individuals, and a new industrial age.

Tapping into the industrial sun will bring untold creativity, new wealth for billions, and a greater quality of life for all souls aboard, including all species dear to this great and fragile earth. The industrial sun is a power supply.

Power, and energy for doing real work such as heating, cooling, powering electronics, and transportation fuels upon which we all depend. Industrial man is now evolving from the "Hydrocarbon Man," into the "Silicon Man." The Green New Deal is all about this human industrial revolution. The evolution from basing industry on Carbon, to basing our industry on Water.

The future of our civilization is based on a change of our energy economics. From a commodity model which has ruled in the industrial age for three centuries, to a self-sufficient model which will unleash and stabilize economies worldwide.

The Green New Deal is about the industrial revolution of sustainability, self-reliance, and economic resilience for America, and all countries.

Chapter One - Global Toxicity

"It happens then as it does to physicians in the treatment of consumption, which in the commencement is easy to cure, and difficult to understand; but when it has neither been discovered in time nor treated upon a proper principle, it becomes easy to understand and difficult to cure. The same thing happens in state affairs, by foreseeing them at a distance, which is only done by men of talents, the evils which might arise from them are soon cured but when, from want of foresight, they are suffered to increase to such a height that they are perceptible to everyone, there is no longer any remedy."

- Machiavelli - The Prince, (1513)

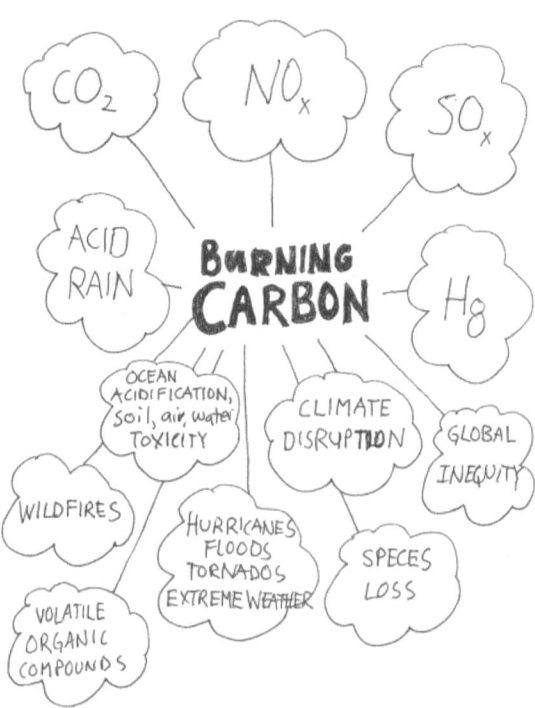

As a civilization we face major categories of impending catastrophe: global toxicity, climate disruption, and energy available only as a commodity, respectively. All of these are caused by burning Carbon.

The first category, toxicity, has been accumulating like a mounting wave about to crash, as three hundred years of burning fossil fuel emissions, and the fever pitch with which we consume and burn carbon today, has stressed the biosphere to a tipping point.

The decade of the 2020s will be the story of us. Do we advance, or do we collapse?

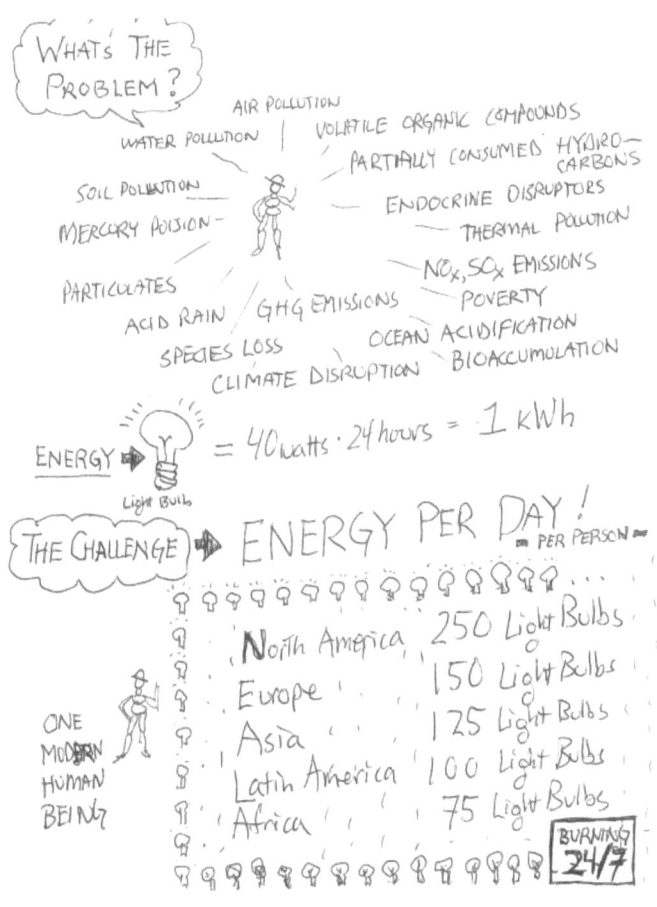

It may be debated how long we can last as a fossil fuel powered civilization, just as we can debate how long anyone can last with the garage door down and a piston engine running, but the conclusion is inevitable. Given enough toxic exposure, we won't survive. Biology under stress either adapts, or dies. The stakes at risk for our industrial future are just that: our future.

The reality is our modern lifestyle requires copious amounts of energy. Using fossil fuels worldwide results in an enormous range of toxic discharge, and economic servitude. Is there a better way? Must we always still use energy based on 1880s technology?

We must advance to an energy system which not only meets world demand, but also moves us in a forward direction with expanded universal access to more energy, more performance, non toxicity, and lower costs than our current fossil fuel system.

We must advance. Poverty is a direct result of non-access to energy. The industrial sun is the path for all people to access real energy, everywhere and everyday. We can obsolete human poverty in our world, but it's going to take technology, and access to energy.

The Green New Deal recognizes this intimate link between energy, environment, economic development, distributed new wealth, job creation and human dignity all intertwined. Get the energy part right, and everything else can happen.

Energy appetites

It takes a lot of energy to power a modern world, let alone a world of 7 billion with modern appetites.

In our modern world, where you live determines the average amount of energy required by every man, woman and child.

Not counting the billions of people who want a modern life style, our current consumption in North America is about 250 kWh of energy per day, per man, woman and child.

The equivalent of powering 250 lightbulbs of 40 watts each 24/7 for each person in North America. They never turn off, they just burn constantly consuming fossil fuels which only result in reoccurring fuel bills each month and vast amounts of waste product polluting our soils, air water and biology.

WHY FOSSIL FUELS ARE BAD

I. TOXIC

II. EXPENSIVE

III. TEARS UP ENVIRONMENT WHERE EXTRACTED, TRANSPORTED, STORED

IV. LIMITED RESOURCE

V. ONLY A FEW CONTROL WHAT IS NEEDED BY ALL

VI. PRICE VOLATILITY

VII. BURNS INCOMPLETE CAUSING CO_2, NO_x, SO_x, VOC, PCH, Hg

VIII. ECONOMIC MOTIVATION FOR DISRUPTION

IX. BIOLOGICAL IMPACTS ON DNA

X. REOCCURRING BILL WHEN USED

XI. ACID RAIN

XII. OCEAN ACIDIFICATION

XIII. CLIMATE DISRUPTION

The Green New deal understands there's a relationship between the local and global crisis we all face: the polluting of our environment to a point where life is not supported.

WHY SOLAR CLEAN FUELS ARE GOOD

I. NON-TOXIC

II. INEXPENSIVE WHEN LEASED

III. MINIMAL IMPACT WHERE USED

IV. AVAILABLE GLOBALLY

V. DISTRIBUTED ACCESS

VI. NO FUEL COSTS

VII. NO COMBUSTION REQUIRED

VIII. ENDS GLOBAL INEQUITY

IX. NO IMPACTS ON DNA

X. NON-COMMODITY BASED ENERGY

XI. NO ACID RAIN

XII. NO OCEAN ACIDIFICATION

XIII. NO CLIMATE DISRUPTION

A Green New Deal is good for America, being good for all countries and economies.

If we want to achieve a world of actual peace and prosperity, then clean energy economics is the power supply for such a world.

Human poverty must be, and can be obsolete with the application of solar power supply and UV water sterilizers for example.

All the world needs to end poverty is an understanding of the hardware required in doing so starting with basic needs such as clean potable water from any source.

Water borne diseases kill over a thousand children worldwide - each day. Use Solar powered UV water sterilizers and the carnage ends. This is the Green New Deal.

The high costs of delivering energy to everyone in the world in quantities sufficient to lift everyone above the poverty level can't be achieved with fossil fuels.

The reality is we can't deliver energy to everyone transporting materials all over the world. Therefore, the Green New Deal taps into an industrial scale energy already distributed: the sun.

America is a leader.

Either we lead the world off the cliff with continued fossil fuels, or forward in history realizing there is nothing more efficient from a life-cycle perspective than a primary power converter of solar energy.

After all, all fossil fuels all started as ancient sunlight. A small portion of ancient solar energy grown biomass was buried and accumulated over the eons.

Over millions of years of underground high temperature and pressure fossil fuels were formed.

OIL IS ANCIENT SUNLIGHT

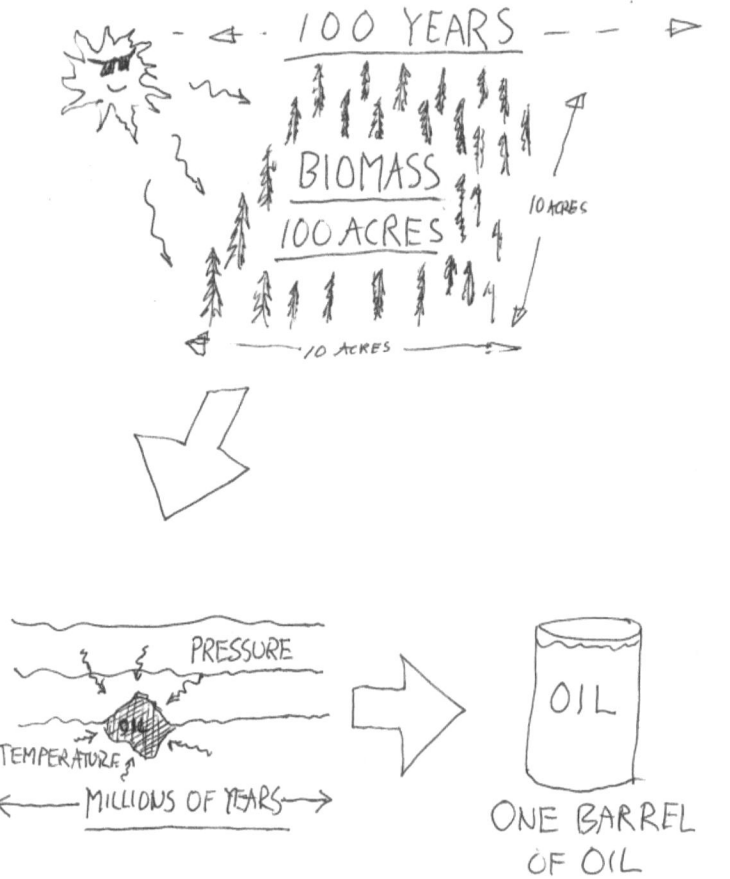

ONE BARREL
OF OIL

Instead of mining the ground for ancient solar resources, we need only turn skyward and harvest enormous amounts of energy directly. We don't need a middleman. Solar energy is delivered everywhere on earth. The fossil fuel problem is toxicity, and ever increasing danger due to bioaccumulation, as complex organisms (including humans) accumulate toxins in their flesh and organs. The continued industrial worldwide burning of fossil fuels is a toxic time bomb. Burning fossil fuels are toxic.

Burning, or more accurately, partially burned hydrocarbons spew a vast array of toxic materials including but not limited to Green House Gases (GHG), NOx, SOX, particulates, Mercury poisoning, partially consumed hydrocarbons (PCH), volatile organic compounds, (VOC), Endocrine Disruptors (ED) and others, having terrible impacts on the soils, air, water, and biology worldwide these toxins disrupt.

Ocean acidification, and acid rain from millions of tons of daily emissions from industrial burning threatens our fisheries, forests and farmlands on all fronts. The oceans are already depleted over 90% of preindustrial levels, and with the increased stress and compromise of millions of tons of plastics accumulating toxins in the food web we're destroying our oceans.

The oceans are the very lungs of life on earth, If our oceans collapse, we collapse. The toxic time bomb of a fossil fuel world is no longer survivable. We are at the tipping point.

Climate Disruption

Language is everything.

If we don't get the language right, how can we possibly solve a global climate crisis? We never get answers better than the questions we ask, so it's vital to first ask the right question.

In the 1970s, the author remembers "Earth Day" bringing attention to our collective "industrial footprint." The toxicity of our industrial life.

Earth day asked questions including how much pollution can our world bear?
In the 1990s, the language evolved to include "global warming," and the "Greenhouse Effect" continuing a process of examining the costs of our "fossil fuel" powered civilization with the millions of tons of emissions each day.

Scientists tracking and reporting the rapid temperature increase of the surface of the earth and oceans began to raise our awareness, still fossil fuel use continued unabated into total domination of energy markets worldwide.

In the early 2000s the language evolved again in an effort to describe the threat of global emissions on natural systems. "Climate change" entered the lexicon as a way to begin talking about the global climate crisis. This phase proves, however, a disservice to the question of industrial toxins affecting soils, biology, air and water worldwide. The phrase "climate change" remains vague, and unfocused.

The weakness of the language "global warming," was exploited when opposition pointed to short-term cooling (disregarding temperatures rising worldwide in a saw-tooth pattern), as another way to cloud the discussion keeping the commercial fossil fuel status quo. The phrase "Climate change," fails to convey a complete understanding of the global climate crisis, being vague, and unfocused as to cause.

Climate change from what? Orbits, volcanism, geology, the thermal Haline ocean circulation of heat, human emissions, there are many factors which may effect a climate change. Each of these phrases leaves the discussion open ended, and nebulous regarding cause, leaving the worldwide crisis only to grow unbounded without solution.

In facing a climate crisis, we need language which is not vague, and is focused on the heart of the issue.

The climate crisis we face is "Climate Disruption."

The phrase climate disruption is clear. We're talking about anthropogenic toxins, we're talking about the pollution our civilization emits now based on fossil fuels and its effect in our environment. Green house gases (GHG) including CO_2 and Methane, NOx, SOx, particulates, mercury, volatile organic compounds (VOC), partially consumed hydrocarbons (PCH), endocrine disruptors, the list of toxins we emit on industrial scale reaching millions of tons each day are now disastrous in effect.

Changing the chemistry of our atmospheres and ocean, increasing the amount of heat in the local environment, unleashing feedback loops such as loss of sea ice, (limiting surface reflection), and disrupting the temperature difference between equator and poles causing the Polar Vortex will only increase in potency without a real solution.

Fossil fuels have powered the industrial world for three centuries, however the 21st century can no longer survive the toxic heat-engines and fuels of the 18th century. Burning fossil fuels makes the entire food web acts like a toxicity concentrator. Phytoplankton absorb these toxins, Zooplankton eat the tainted algae and bio-concentrate these toxins accumulating in their flesh and organs. Small fish eat the Zooplankton, big fish eat the small fish, and the biggest fish - we eat.

Each step of this nefarious cycle brings the toxins front and center into our lives on a cumulative basis. If we continue to spew pollution, system collapse will at some point be inescapable. We are reaching this point.

Climate Disruption wasn't a process created solely by our present generation, we stand on centuries of industrial pollution. The challenge and legacy of this generation will be what do we do now? The activities we engage in which load our atmosphere and oceans, our soils, air, waters, and biologies with toxicities upon which our entire life depends now threaten the global ecosystem.

The Green New Deal allows us to address this elephant in the room. Climate Disruption allows us to focus on the real questions.

How can we power our civilization without fossil fuels? How do we evolve our civilization away from burning Carbon? How do we obsolete the toxic flow of materials which is disrupting planet earth. The answer: industrial revolution moving beyond a "world of combustion" into a world of solar clean fuels and the Fuel Cell. A Green New Deal for planet earth.

Not less energy for everyone, but more. Not just an alternative to how we do things, rather something better. The question is how can we power our basic machines better than we do today? With more energy, no toxicity, universal availability not limited to any one place, or any one hole in the ground. How can we power our most basic engines for transportation, electricity generation, and chemical fuels without toxicity? Can the 21st century move beyond the 19th century in energy technology?

Can a new economy be built promoting jobs, and economic prosperity across the country? Yes. And, by mobilizing the Green New Deal, done with a profit.

Chapter Two -
Energy and the Economy

"... And when Alexander saw the breadth of his domain,... he wept... For there were no more worlds to conquer"

- Plutarch - (circa. 79 AD)

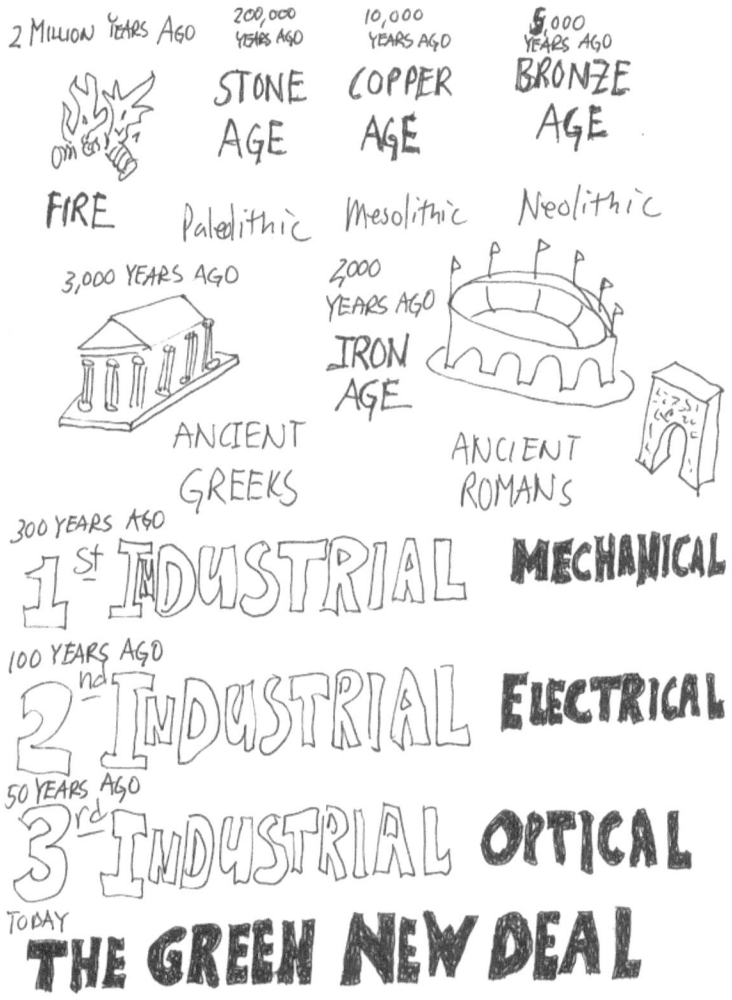

Up until the 21st century human civilization has always been powered by combustion.

Before the beginning of the industrial age stretching back into deep time the fuel of choice for civilization was wood, and charcoal derived from wood.

Through the ages from our earliest use of fire, through the long Stone Age and Copper Age of the Neolithic, into the Bronze and Iron ages, our civilizations have marched with the increasing advances of energy density, and the new materials and capabilities new material science brought.

For the ancient Greeks, and Romans, wood, and charcoal derived from wood, were the energy industry of the age, and vital to the empire. It takes a lot of fuel for empire building.

The ancient Greeks thrived during the "Bronze Age" where increasingly hot furnaces and advancing technology ushered in the alloy Bronze which totally transformed the world. Vastly stronger than Copper alone which dominated the earlier "Copper Age" itself a great leap over stone tools, Bronze was an industrial revolution improving farming implements, tools, and most significantly weapons. Industrial revolution and social implications were off and running.

Energy supply became a problem, however, early on for the Greeks, who suffered their own "energy crisis" by the 4th century B.C. It took a lot of wood to power Greek society.

Market demand for wood caused massive deforestation in ancient Greece causing the erosion of fertile soils further stressing the farming and grazing in rural Greece.

Equipping Bronze Age armies with weapons required enormous smelting operations. The fuel needed for daily cooking, heating, and lighting all required an industrial amount of wood to constantly be sought, found, defended, cut, loaded and transported back to the city states. The ancients faced their energy crisis almost daily as the appetites for energy increased exponentially with population growth, and fueled the growth of empire. Wood was a limited resource facing increasing demand each day.

Oak, the wood most cherished for charcoal was deforested out of Greece by the 4th Century B.C. So vital were olive trees it was decreed a death sentence to chop down an olive tree for charcoal production. Even thousands of years ago civilization had to grapple with their "modern" need for fuels, and the ecological devastation industrial power supply seemingly demands.

It doesn't take long for ten thousand humans to consume a lot of wood during the Bronze age, imagine 100,000 people? A million? Wood was a valuable commodity, and represented the energy Industry of the ancient Greeks. Energy was vital to the Greek military (taking lots of wood to make Triremes), and enormous amounts of wood and charcoal for smelting, cooking, heating, and lighting for growing populations and military campaigns.

The appetite for energy of any civilization grows as it does. The ancient Greeks ran out of local fuel and eventually collapsed. The Romans ran out of fuel for their outstretched military, and also collapsed. We can take a lesson from history and choose a 21st century power supply which won't run out, and is available to all, and will never collapse: the sun.

Deforestation was a major catastrophe for the ancient Greeks, and every civilization which followed. Plato wrote poems of lament as the forests around his beloved Ithaca, and the Athenian forests were cut down for fuel and decimated "...only the bones of the earth remain... where only the bees can survive." Energy supplies are vital, and energy's impact on civilizations are evident and dominate from the beginning.

The essential relationship between energy and civilization is absolute.

It's no coincidence the ancient Greek, then Roman empires collapsed in no small part to a lack of energy access having outpaced their ability to provide basic energy required for all aspects of life both domestic and military.

In Roman times, nearly the entire Italian peninsula was deforested by the 2nd century B.C. By the 1st century B.C.

Rome was importing wood from over a thousand miles away, as far away as the Caucasus.

By the the 3rd century AD Rome was in such need of wood to fuel the Roman military campaigns and domestic demands for energy a military fleet was formed called "naviculari lignarii" (literally wood ships) and launched to retrieve wood from far afield to import wood into Rome by force if necessary. An entire military industrial complex in ancient Rome was secured to insure a source of Carbon fuel. In their case wood. In our case?

Our modern civilization in principle is no different. In fact, our reliance on energy in the modern age is unbridled and even more critical to the daily survival and modern life of people. This essential relationship between energy and industry, and empire is as potent today under fossil fuels as it has always been. The Green New Deal recognizes the industrial opportunity of modern technology applied to our most essential industrial need: energy. And, with a clean energy paradigm we can address and solve the 17 global environmental crises we face by recognizing the common thread: all of our problems come from burning carbon.

The Green New Deal recognizes the opportunity for addressing major problems including global toxicity, inequity, and poverty by addressing the fundamental connection between energy, environment and economics. If you have a source of energy which is stable, cost effective, and productive, then you have a resilient means of production and sustained growth. If your source of energy is non-toxic in use, then there are no toxic liabilities and impacts which can harm anything or anyone.

Does such a energy paradigm exist? Yes. Solar clean energy fuels.

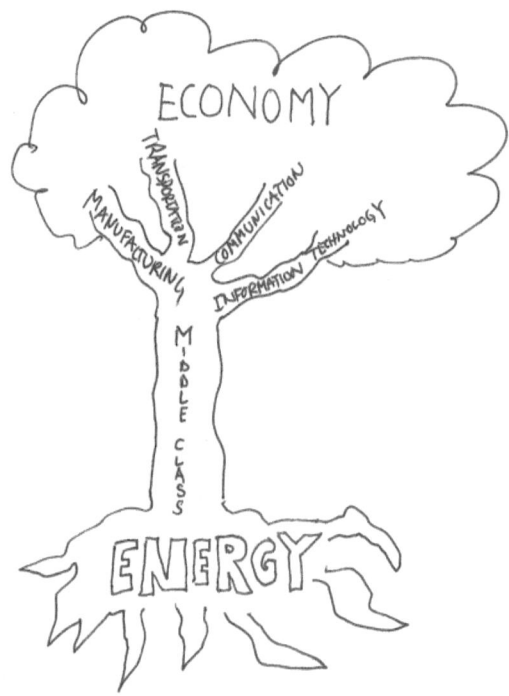

An economy is like a tree. With strong roots a tree can be defoliated and still recover. However, with weak roots even the slightest stress can be catastrophic. For our economy, the root of the tree is energy.

If energy is available the roots can be strong.

If energy is not available for the roots, then the tree cannot be sustained. The trunk of our economic tree is the middle class. The laborers and consumers of the modern economy. The trunk needs the roots to provide daily energy for activity and growth.

Out in the major branches are all of the categories of economic activity we do in modern economies including manufacturing, communications, electronics, transportation, services, and others all branching further out into more and more energy demands of our economy.

A healthy economy requires healthy roots. Healthy roots, require reliable access to energy. The Green New Deal develops access to the most powerful power supply we have: our daily sun.

Solar energy falling on the earth, not buried in the earth, is the power supply capable of keeping our roots well nourished, and our economy strong, productive, and growing for centuries to come.

Chapter Three -
Energy and Industrial Revolution

"This goodly frame, the Earth, seems to me a sterile promontory; This most excellent canopy, the air, look you, this brave o'er hanging firmament, this majestic roof fretted with golden fire, why it appears no other thing to me than a foul and pestilent congregation of vapors"

- Shakespeare's Hamlet - (Act 2 scene 2)

	FUEL	ENGINE
18th CENTURY	COAL	STEAM
19th CENTURY	OIL	INTERNAL COMBUSTION
20th CENTURY	NATURAL GAS AVIATION FUEL	TURBINE
21st CENTURY	HYDROGEN	FUEL CELLS

THE EVOLUTION
OF REVOLUTION

Energy, is everything to life, and to economic health.

If you command energy resources, then all of the fundamental elements of industry can thrive: manufacturing, transportation, communications, building heating ventilation air conditioning (HVAC), electronics, agriculture, construction, to name a few all thrive at the need of energy.

As the roots of the economic tree, command of energy is vital for economic stability and sustained growth. Since economy (products and services) require energy if we get this right, we have a great future ahead for humanity. Get energy wrong?

Toxic collapse is inevitable, given every major trend of failing species, acidification of our soils, air and waterways, degradation of our DNA, and increasing climate disruption. Our industrial reliance on fossil fuels has now reached the breaking point for our environment, and it's time to make a fundamental change in energy - we need an industrial evolution in energy.

An industrial revolution recognized by the Green New Deal: industrial sustainability.

A transition from toxicity to non-toxicity. A transition from high and volatile energy costs to no energy costs using distributed solar energy captured, used or stored to be dispatched on demand. In the 21st century, we have the technology.

Three centuries ago we entered the 1st Industrial Revolution and the "energy density" of our engines over human or animal muscle increased 10,000 fold. The power and energy advantages of the Steam Engine compared to human or animal muscle, and even water wheels and wind mills began our industrial ages three centuries ago and launched humanity into a surge of creativity and technology unknown in our entire experience.

An explosion of creativity and job creation happened as industrialism took hold. The economic and social impacts for Americans, and all societies worldwide, was shaken to the core over the last centuries as the country shifted from agrarian to urban as we began to evolve our long march into modern life.

Energy, and specifically, the "energy density" of fuels made all the difference, just as it does today.

Consider the numbers from a thermodynamic perspective.

The specific energy density of burning wood is about 16 MJ/Kg. The ancients increased the energy density by manufacturing Charcoal from wood increasing its energy density nearly to coal at around 30 MJ/Kg. Transporting charcoal was much easier than bulk wood, and was highly prized.

To make charcoal the ancients would cut down trees, and dig a big pit. The trees were loaded into the pit and set ablaze. As soon as the fire took hold they'd cover the wood with dirt, and wait. After some time, from days to weeks depending on conditions, a transformation would occur. The buried wood limited the oxygen available, slowing down combustion lowering the temperature of this combustion creating a condition where impurities and moisture find their way out of the wood. This process to "pyrolyse" concentrates the amount of Carbon (and therefore the Hydrogen attached to the Carbon) and increases the energy density of the fuel.

Three hundred years ago, the 1st Industrial Revolution was fueled by Coal, which has a specific energy density of approximately 30 MJ/Kg depending on the type of coal you measure.

History, through our industrial ages connects the Energy Density of our fuels with the types of engines we can use, and a series of industrial revolutions ensue all moving our civilization forward as the energy density in fuels increase.

As fuels become more energy dense industrial revolution is soon to follow.

The 18th Century

During the 1700s the fuel leap of the century was coal over wood.

The 1st Industrial Revolution unleashed early steam engines and transformed the world commercially, socially, and politically. The first generation of steam engines constructed to pump water out of coal mines used a single piston in a cylinder heated from the outside using coal as the fuel.

Coal powered steam engines were originally called "External Combustion" engines as the combustion was done outside of the working cylinder. Early steam engines were also called "Atmospheric Engines" because the power stroke was not from the steam injected into the cylinder pushing a piston for power. Rather, steam was injected under the piston to lift the unloaded piston into the up position.

As soon as the piston was at its highest point, the steam valve was closed and a cold water injection valve opened. The immediate cooling by the water sprayed under the piston caused the air to condense rapidly, resulting in a rapid partial vacuum forming under the piston.

The rapid cooling and partial vacuum under the piston allowed the weight of the atmosphere above the piston to literally "push" down on the piston and the power stroke occurs.

Imagine an old fashioned hand powered water pump. The hand crank is on a pivot such that your "push" down on the leaver causes the other end to go up. This "up" stroke pulls up the plunger submerged in the mine and draws up the water. Hence, an Atmospheric engine, as the power stroke was from the weight of the air pushing down, just as your hand on an old fashioned hand pump.

As 1699 turned into 1700, Newcomen's early steam engine unleashed the course of industry, and set in motion an entirely new chapter in human history: our industrial age. Technology, and the social changes it brought transformed not only the American economy but the world economy, as humanity became industrial, and all the social advancement so unleashed.

By the mid 1750's James Watt made the technological breakthrough which propelled the steam engine out of the mines and into "distributed" applications. Watt realized instead of repeatedly heating and cooling one cylinder it's more efficient to have a "boiler" always hot, and a "condenser" always cold, and use a working fluid (water) between them.

Heat water to steam, push a piston, then condense the left over steam back into water (allowing it to absorb heat again) to be fed back to the boiler and the working cycle repeats. Watt's new improved steam engine again inspired revolution.

Consider the American revolution of 1776. Is it a coincidence the great political accomplishment and social leap of the American Constitution was created just as an Industrial revolution appears? The 1st Industrial Revolution, unleashed by the power of coal transformed America not only from a technological perspective, it unleashed the great social advancement of individual political rights, improved factory and living conditions, individual rights, an advancement of the American constitution unseen anywhere in the world.

Industrial revolution in any age unleashes economic and social frontiers.

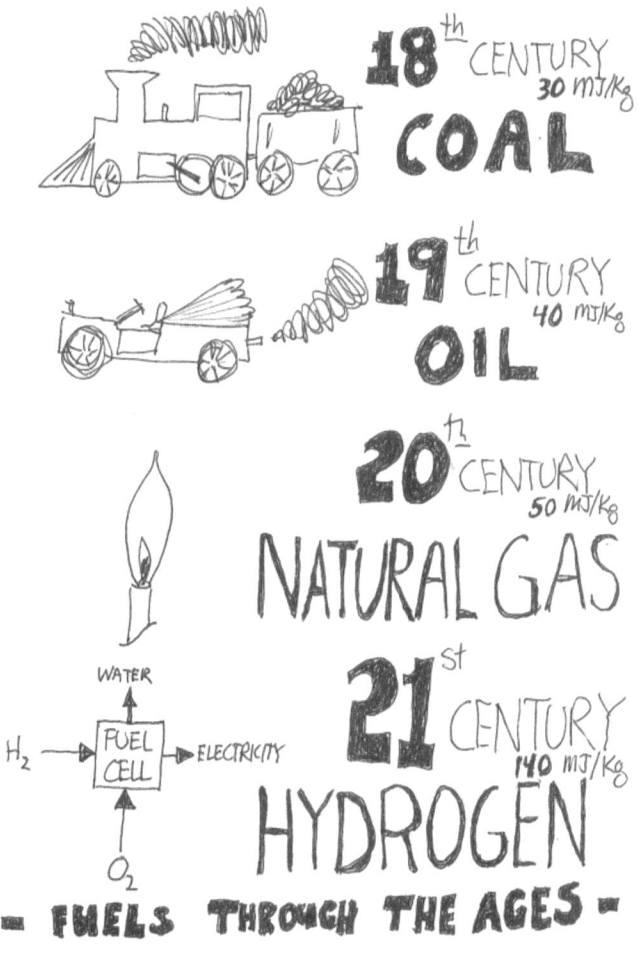

18th CENTURY 30 mJ/kg
COAL

19th CENTURY 40 mJ/kg
OIL

20th CENTURY 50 mJ/kg
NATURAL GAS

WATER

H₂ → FUEL CELL → ELECTRICITY

O₂

21st CENTURY 140 mJ/kg
HYDROGEN

- FUELS THROUGH THE AGES -

The 1st Industrial Revolution enabled a new level of capitalism, just as each industrial revolution to follow. As a revolution, steam engines can be used to power anything, anywhere, no longer tied to a particular river or stream as early water wheels powered early America.

Industrial revolution means economic stimulus and entrepreneurship across all sectors of economy and across all social classes. Industrial revolution is good for economics, and for increased social justice.

The toxic costs of industrialism based on carbon

There was a high price to pay on health for industrialization, namely massive amounts of pollution. The term "acid rain" and "smog" were coined in the early 1800s as even then, London and other places choked on toxic emissions from industry. Considered the cost of progress, people endured as their health, and the health of their downwind livestock and farmlands all suffered.

What we can learn from the energy density of fuels?

From a technological perspective, the 1st Industrial Revolution was made possible because the energy density of fuel went from food calories for muscle power burning inside living cells, or burning wood, to machines burning coal for powering steam engines thousands of times more powerful.

During the 18th century, the fuel of the industrial revolution was coal: King Coal.

The 19th Century

The Energy revolution of the 19th century was powered by Petroleum and the rise of Big Oil. Coal has an energy density of around 30 MJ/Kg depending on the type of coal. Petroleum has an energy density of around 40 MJ/Kg.

This increased fuel density may seem modest, however, the energy density of fuels going from solids to liquids have dramatic impacts making a revolution in engine technology possible, and changed the world again.

The energy available from oil, increased the energy density and therefore the power density of engines which transformed the 19th Century with the advent of "internal combustion" engines leaps and bounds in performance over "external combustion" engines of the previous century.

In the 19th Century, the fuel of industrial revolution was Oil.

The old steam engines produced heat outside of the working cylinder. Now, with internal combustion also called an "explosion engine" heat was released inside the working cylinder to work the piston directly.

As external combustion Steam Engines could power heavy locomotives and heavy ships, now Internal combustion engines could power a wide range of lighter vehicles.

The "modern car" was invented by Karl Benz circa. 1878. Today's piston engine cars, are just an incremental improvement on everything Karl Benz demonstrated in the 1870s.

With over 88 million new Internal Combustion Engine (ICE) cars being sold each year as of this writing, Karl Benz would be amazed to see we still use essentially the same engines he used 150 years ago.

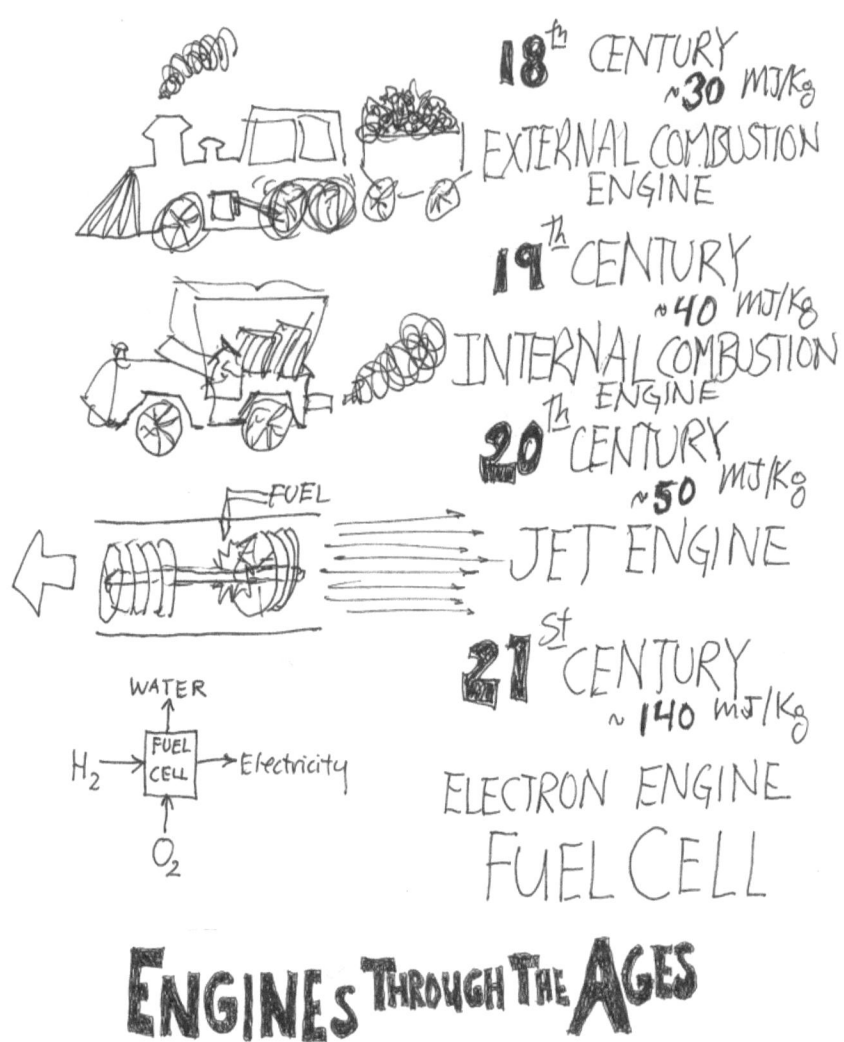

18th CENTURY ~30 mJ/kg
EXTERNAL COMBUSTION ENGINE

19th CENTURY ~40 mJ/kg
INTERNAL COMBUSTION ENGINE

20th CENTURY ~50 mJ/kg
JET ENGINE

21st CENTURY ~140 mJ/kg
ELECTRON ENGINE
FUEL CELL

FUEL

WATER

H_2 → FUEL CELL → Electricity

O_2

ENGINEs THROUGH THE AGES

Internal combustion engines were transformative, not only in the physical powers of man to use engines to power cars, motorcycles, trucks, small boats and other power demands, the 19th century industrial revolution not only transformed transportation for the masses, it changed American culture. Personal freedom of travel and lifestyle, greater energy density in fuels unleashed our American way of life.

The last few decades of the 1800s was changing America, and the world, in leaps and bounds even then unimagined. The telegraph, the early telephone, the automobile, photography, these are revolutionary jumps of technology, all made possible by liquid fuels (oil distillates) and their higher energy density.

The 19th century also saw a new energy player and revolution emerge which sent the fossil fuel industry reeling coming online - electricity.

In 1892, the world changed again. Industrial revolution was about to unleash our modern life, and more than anything before, to empower individuals - the electric age.

The 1st Industrial Revolution came up against the 2nd Industrial Revolution where electricity and the petroleum waves crashed into each other.

From the 1860s John D. Rockefeller consolidated his oil empire often through ruthless means. Over the 30 years from the 1860s through 1892 Rockefeller had amassed an enormous fortune selling Kerosine for lamp oil. The future always looked bright to Mr. Rockefeller as he extended his monopoly on Kerosine lighting fluid through the decades up to 1892 throughout the world.

A can of Standard Oil's Kerosine was the same high quality from Beijing to New York City. Then, in 1892 something happened.

For thirty years since the 1860s rock oil was used as a raw material from which Kerosine was distilled. Kerosine was a revolutionary advancement in lighting.

The first life of the oil industry was improving an age old problem for humanity: indoor lighting. The oil industry in the beginning was in the lighting fluid business with the amazing distillation of Kerosine from rock oil. Cars didn't yet exist, gasoline, as a byproduct of Kerosine production was often dumped into nearby streams and rivers as waste.

In 1892, however, the world changed in an instant with the electric light. In a flash Rockefeller was suddenly at the threshold of ruin. In 1892-93 the International Exposition at the Chicago's World Fair changed the world forever. Electricity had arrived.

During this international exposition Tesla and Westinghouse beat out Edison's DC current winning the contract to light the entire exposition and fairgrounds. It was spectacular. The electric light and AC power to distribute electricity to far reaches promised to totally transform the lighting industry. And, it did. Imagine coming from a world of candles, animal fats, and at last Kerosine only to see electric light for the first time?

In one night, with the flip of a switch, Rockefeller's business was rendered obsolete. Who would buy Kerosine, if they could just flip a switch for light? Rockefeller was facing ruin. In one night, Kerosine, and John D. Rockefeller were all at once sidelined. Industrial revolution isn't welcomed by everyone. Representing the establishment Rockefeller was rocked to his core.

In perhaps the most remarkable pivot in industrial history, Rockefeller realized there was a way out. A new path to forge and new world's to conquer. There was a way to save his entire business, and not only save it, but find a new market worth many times Kerosine ever was!

Rockefeller's great realization?

Change the distilleries from Kerosine, to Gasoline. Rockefeller pulled off the biggest pivot in industrial history abandoning the lighting market which to date had been his bread and butter, to embrace this new fangled internal combustion engine (ICE) and the new market of liquid powered transportation. Gasoline would be Rockefeller's new rising star.

Rockefeller showed remarkable insight, and applied himself with all his focus. In the 1890s there were three major technologies available to power automobiles, steam power, electric power, and internal combustion, respectively. Market share was about one third each in 1899, at the turn of the new century.

The first car dealership ever opened, indeed only carried electric cars. A gasoline powered car was the immediate winner. The rapid expansion of AC electricity insured there were far more electric charging stations available than places to buy gasoline in 1899.

By 1905, one third of all police cars in NYC were electric powered with charging stations throughout New York City. A fleet of over 400 electric taxis plied their trade in the turn of the century streets of New York. To most people, including Edison working on his own electric car, the future was electric.

Rockefeller, to make his new plan work, needed to make sure the only cars being purchased were gasoline powered cars. By 1904, electric cars were still the best sellers.

Rockefeller, well versed in taking a market by any and all means, set his evil genius to transforming the world in his image following his view of selling the greatest commodity anyone could ever imagine: rock oil. Transforming the oil industry from lighting to transportation was the plot of the century. Rockefeller's plan?

The world will be powered by gasoline, and the world will buy their gasoline from Standard Oil.

This moment in industrial history is monumental not only for Standard Oil, it was pivotal for social progress as it unleashed the machine age in earnest and all of the social stresses such growth entails. A new era in militarism was launched on liquid engines. Those who controlled energy resources, best controlled the outcome of war.

Rockefeller was in a unique position as he launched his new effort to secure the future of internal combustion engines burning gasoline.

Making his first fortune selling groceries to the Union Army during the civil war, Rockefeller was well versed in selling commodities to the government. He knew the purchase power of the government and lobbied vigorously for the military to transition away from horses and purchase internal combustion engines running on gasoline. Gasoline supplied by Standard Oil.

Rockefeller, as no other force could, took command of the enormous emerging energy markets and set off to sell the greatest "commodity" the world had every seen. After all, what could be more profitable than selling energy liquids, which as soon as they're used, require the customer to buy again!

Oil became the industrial drug, and no industry in human history commanded such redistribution of resources as the enormous appetite for energy in America with money flowing from consumer to producer. Selling gasoline worldwide grew leaps and bounds with unimagined profits flowing into Rockefeller's coffers. Rockefeller had figured out a way to tap into the very life blood of economies - charge them all for the energy they use, and after they use it, charge them again.

Under Rockefeller, not only would America and world transportation burn his gasoline, all of the militaries of the world would do so too. The stage was set. World War I was the ignition and a pattern of using and securing fossil fuels was baked into the cake. Fossil fuels would power the American economy, and it would power the world. Oil, would fuel World War I.

Standard Oil profits from World War I propelled Rockefeller into the richest man who ever lived.

Rudolf Diesel

As a side bar it's important to comment on the story of Rudolf Diesel. Books have been written, and more could be written on the fate of Rudolf Diesel.

In the 1890s another innovation in internal combustion engines came to be with Rudolf Diesel's invention known as his namesake Diesel engine. Gasoline powered internal combustion engines of the 1890s are not entirely efficient or powerful. Adequate for small engine needs, it became apparent in the 1890s there are significant power limitations to the gasoline engines of the day.

Heavy trucks, and other large loads struggled using gasoline engines.

Gasoline's limitations would be dangerously apparent in large marine vessels at sea. Gasoline was a dangerous fuel for marine applications being highly volatile, constantly moved about by the boats motion the volatile fumes had a tendency to collect below decks. The slightest spark caused explosions.

Diesel engines don't use a spark ignition, but rather a "compression" ignition. Using precision machined pistons the high compression of the fuel and air mixture inside the piston causes the ignition at the top of the stroke. Using a less volatile fuel mixture, the Diesel engine with compression ignition allowed a wide range of less volatile fuels to be used instead of gasoline.

Diesel engines were the original "flex" fuel engines. They could use many fuel types, especially biofuels. Using diesel engines any nation could grow their own fuels.

Indeed, a Diesel engine would work with most natural oils including peanut, soybean and vegetable oils. This brings us to the intersection of Diesel and Rockefeller.

Diesel, towards the end of the 1890s began a series of lectures and articles promoting his superior Diesel engine for applications requiring more powerful engines such as tractors, trucks, marine vessels, and even power stations turning Tesla's new AC generators.

Rudolf Diesel demonstrated his versatile engine across Europe and to America showing his engine for powering factories and heavy vehicles, trucks, and tractors running on Peanut oil which could be grown by every farmer.

Later in his life Diesel was outspoken against the increasing tensions for war before World War I, and advocated for countries to grow their own fuel using his Diesel engines as a means of lessening energy dependency among countries.

Rudolf Diesel wanted to give the world his engine for peace, reducing the dependence on Standard Oil, or any third party, for liquid fuels.

To Diesel, the world could be prosperous and inherently stable for all countries using locally grown biofuels and with his Diesel engine could be energy independent and prosperous. A century ago the world could have turned to biofuels.

Diesel pointed out, if farmers used diesel powered tractors and heavy machinery they could grow their own fuel, (Peanuts and other legumes are also terrific for re-Nitrification of the soils) they'd be essentially energy independent - lowering their costs and increasing their profit.

Diesel envisioned an industrial world of peace based on industrial energy independence for all countries reducing the military stress he saw taking over the world. There was a moment a century ago when the world could have taken a different path.

Rockefeller, however, would have none of it.

As international tensions grew towards World War I, a financial windfall stood before Standard Oil supplying petroleum products to the US Military and allies for the impending conflict.

On the eve of war, Rudolf Diesel mysteriously disappeared overboard from a ferry boat crossing the English channel. There are many speculations on why, and how he disappeared off the boat. The official line is suicide, which as an inventor the author can attest is nonsense. Diesel was living for his inventions, he was on his way to London to sign a large technology transfer deal to the Royal Navy to use Diesel engines on English U-boats, worth hundreds of thousands of pounds.

Some historians point to German nationalists who didn't want Diesel to give his engine technology to the Royal Navy for powering U-boats, as he was traveling to London to do as a suspect. Others, point to mounting debts which drove Diesel to suicide which doesn't really follow as he was on his way to sign a large deal with the Royal Navy.

Who had the most to gain from the death of Diesel?

John D. Rockefeller. Coincidence? Rockefeller has long demonstrated violent and ruthless tactics in business. Would it be a stretch to eliminate one of the greatest threats to his growing empire? After all, Diesel was telling countries they could grow their own fuel. Rockefeller was at war, and in war there are casualties.

Soon after Diesel's death at sea, Rockefeller named his formulation for a less volatile fuel than gasoline he called "Diesel" fuel. Not Diesel fuel from biofuels and organic sources promoting local and global stability as Rudolf Diesel advocated, but "Diesel" fuel from petroleum distillates formulated to work in his engines. Fuel from rock oil. Rockefeller's way.

By the outbreak of World War I the dye was cast. Standard Oil and the organization of the Standard Oil Company demonstrated vast wealth can be controlled and accumulated by those controlling specific holes in the ground, distillation facilities and distribution of liquid fuels supported and defended by local militaries. As long as sources and downstream distillation of Oil can be controlled, then the vase riches of selling the oil can be restricted to a powerful few.

Corporations, and nations have followed this business model ever sense. Holes in the ground, surrounded by men with guns was the battle cry and the ensuing 20th century became the most violent century in human history enduring two world wars and hundreds of military conflicts.

The 20th Century

Energy in the 20th century took another leap in energy density unleashing another new round of technology, fuels, engines and social freedoms.

We've seen coal in the 18th century with an energy density of 30 MJ/Kg. In the 19th century oil emerges and lifts the energy density of fuels to 40 MJ/Kg making possible internal combustion engines unleashing many industries from automobiles to airplanes.

In the 20th century another step in energy density of fuels emerges with expanded use of natural gas, and aviation fuels which bring us now to 50 MJ/Kg.

At 50 MJ/Kg even more powerful and efficient engines can be produced. Just as distillates brought us gasoline from oil, advancements in distillation brought us aviation fuels ideal for the Jet engine. In the 20th century the energy dense fuels allow Turbines to be used instead of Pistons of the earlier century.

Again, technology based on improving energy density of fuels unleashes a new age of engine efficiency, power and usefulness.

In aviation the new Jet Engine obsoletes the piston engine from the start for most missions.

Before World War II every expert in the aviation world would tell you there is only way to power a heavy aircraft: a piston engine.

All airplanes, since Kitty Hawk used piston engines with liquid fuels. The increased energy density of liquid fuels made these engines powerful enough, and with new materials light enough for powering heaver than air flight.

Before World War II every aviation expert would have emphatically told you "the Only way it can be done, (powering a heavy aircraft) will be done by piston engines... and anything else anyone tells you is complete hokum."

After World War II and the introduction of Jets every expert in the nation, including every civilian would tell you Jets are the future. Before the jet engine, everyone believed pistons were the only way to go. After the jet engine everyone knows the future of speed and power is in jet engines not pistons.

The same parallel is happening today.

The Oil industry says we'll always use piston engines. The Automotive industry say, we're abandoning gasoline piston engines and going electric.

The decade of the 2020s will see a similar transformation where piston engines in cars will be phased out for the higher performance and less expensive Electric Vehicle (EV).

EVs are better than piston engines. By any metric the electrification of transportation is inevitable based on the overwhelming benefits for the consumer.

Piston engines, though still have their uses and missions, were obsolete in terms of military and commercial aircraft post WWII.

After World War II Jet engines have grown to transport over 2 million people at any given moment around the world. Over 2 million people are flying worldwide as you read these words - on jet turbines not pistons.

Can anyone estimate the impact of Jet technology on our modern world? Our modern society?

We are at such a cross roads now, as the world of the 1800s is crashing into the needs of a 21st century. Another energy revolution is afoot. The industrial revolution of sustainability.

The 21st Century

The next industrial step is to move up to solar produced hydrogen fuels and the fuel cell engines.

GLOBAL TOXICITY

GLOBAL FREEDOM

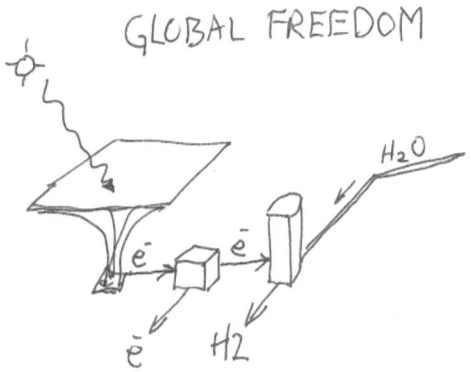

In the 21st century we have an unimaginable world. Magically bring anyone back from history and transport them somehow into our world. What would they think? We fly through the air, talk into boxes with people on the other side of the world in real time, electricity, computers, supermarkets, media, on every front certainly our world of technology would be fantastic and unimaginable to anyone from an earlier age, even just a few decades ago let alone centuries.

The same is true of clean energy if people dismiss it out of hand we're only acting like our friends from history unable to believe the incredible reality of technology in our world today. Undoubtedly, anyone from history would likely find our daily technology unbelievable.

> "... technology sufficiently advanced would be indistinguishable from magic."

> - Arthur C. Clarke -

In the 21st century we have the technology and manufacturing to take industrial power into a new age using solar produced hydrogen fuel from water (also known for 150 years), and Fuel Cell engines to power our motors with greater efficiency and power. Cars, trucks, tractors, buses, trains, construction equipment, farming equipment, heavy equipment and power plants, respectively, can all be powered with greater performance using fuel cell engines not too different than the fuel cells used on the Apollo missions of the 1960s.

The Green New Deal

A Green New Deal is good for America because it recognizes the inherent bond between energy and economy. Get energy right, and the economy can grow. Get energy wrong, and we'll continue to see collapse in our fisheries, farmlands, fields, wetlands, and forests.

Fossil fuels have two major problems: toxicity and high cost. The New Green Deal addresses each by understanding the two are related. They result from one fundamental fact: we burn Carbon. It's time to evolve. Recognizing we don't need Carbon at all in our energy mix solves all of these issues in one fundamental stroke. No Green House Gases, no NOx, SOx, Mercury, particulates and other toxic streams, this is why a new energy economy is sorely needed.

Chapter Four - What's the best fuel?

"I believe that Water will one day be employed as fuel, that Hydrogen and Oxygen, which constitute it, used singly or together, will furnish an inexhaustible source of heat & Light, of which Coal is not capable."

- Jules Verne - The Mysterious Island

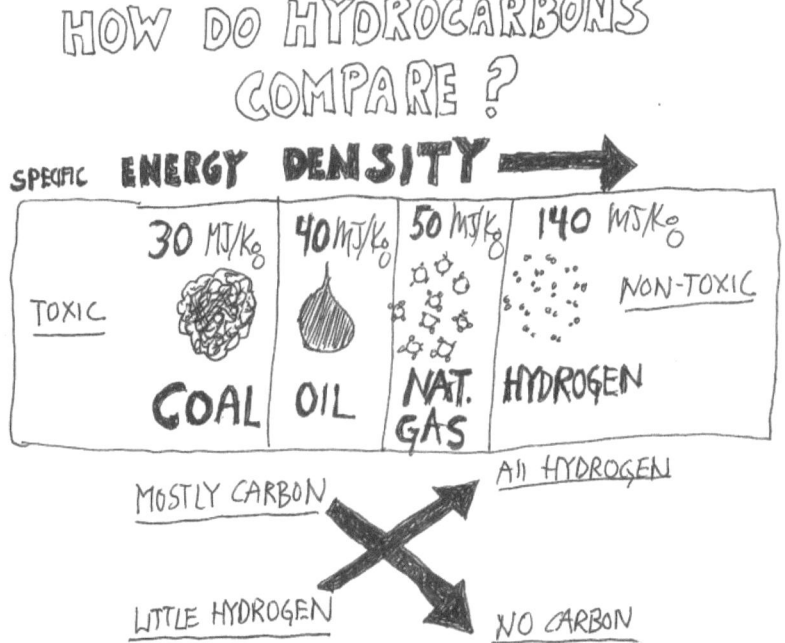

HOW DO HYDROCARBONS COMPARE ?

SPECIFIC ENERGY DENSITY ⟶

TOXIC	30 MJ/kg	40 MJ/kg	50 MJ/kg	140 MJ/kg NON-TOXIC
	COAL	OIL	NAT. GAS	HYDROGEN

MOSTLY CARBON   All HYDROGEN

LITTLE HYDROGEN   NO CARBON

THE ENERGY IS IN THE HYDROGEN

(NOT THE CARBON)

How would we do it? How do we actually power the world with all of the energy we need? Science has an answer.

Any real solution would need to be superior to our existing energy paradigm in every way. Hydrocarbons (fossil fuels) are molecules of Hydrogen and Carbon.

The less Carbon and more Hydrogen by proportion the higher the specific energy density. The energy is in the Hydrogen, not the Carbon. It's always been in the Hydrogen.

We have a hydrogen economy now, but we call it a Carbon economy because we source our carbon (with hydrogen stuck to it) from under the ground, and from around the world, all the while ignoring if we source our hydrogen from water we don't need the carbon at all!

Industrial revolutions do not happen backward, they happen forward.

As we've seen with fuel energy density, industrial evolution has marched forward with increasing energy density from Coal at 30 MJ/Kg, to Oil at 40 MJ/Kg, then Natural Gas and Aviation fuels coming in around 50 MJ/Kg.

Following this historic trend, wouldn't the next fuel innovation need to surpass 50 MJ/Kg in specific energy density? Yes.

If the criteria for the best fuel are power, non-toxicity, availability, and safety then we can look to science for some answers.

WHAT'S THE BEST FUEL ?

LIST ALL FUELS, THEN SORT

WHAT'S TOP OF THE LIST ?

HYDROGEN

POWER SPECIFIC ENERGY DENSITY (MJ/Kg)	NON TOXICITY H_2O	AVAILABLE RESOURCE H_2O	SAFETY NO DEATHS
HYDROGEN (140) ⋮ METHANE PROPANE GASOLINE DIESEL METHANOL ETHANOL ⋮	HYDROGEN ⋮ CO_2 CH_4 NO_x SO_x H_2O ⋮	HYDROGEN ⋮ 70% OF EARTH's SURFACE FEEDSTOCK	HYDROGEN ⋮ LIGHTER THAN AIR HYDROCARBONS HEAVIER THAN AIR

The future needs energy, and lots of it. The best fuel would need to be powerful, so let's look at science and list all the know fuels.

List all of the fuels known to science, and do a simple sort.

Our criteria for sorting will be the criteria required for an Ideal fuel, which is to ask and answer the question "What's the best Fuel?"

Power. Certainly an energy solution would need to be more powerful than fossil fuels. Let's sort the column and list all fuels with the most powerful, the most exothermic, the most KiloCalories per Mole, or MJ per Kg, or any other measure of energy at the top of the list, and we'll get our first answer. What's the most powerful fuel? Sort. Top of the list: Hydrogen.

Hydrogen has an energy density of over 140 MJ/Kg far superior to fuels of the 18th, 19th, and 20th centuries, respectively. Certainly powerful, and consistent with our historical trend of fuel specific energy density increasing at each industrial revolution. Evolution goes up. The most powerful fuel known to science is Hydrogen.

Second question. The best fuel would need to be Non-toxic to solve global toxicity. Let's sort our list of fuels by toxicity of combustion products, with the least toxic on top. Sort. Top of the list: Hydrogen.

Burn Hydrogen and you get Hydrogen-oxide, plain old water. The fact is burn the most powerful fuel, and you get the most benign substance known: water. Isn't the natural world amazing? Water, which covers most of the earth, and the material from which we are mostly made, is the key to the most powerful fuel know to science, and the key to sustainability in the industrial world. How extraordinary is nature, that the result of the most powerful combustion known to science is energy and water.

Hydrogen is totally non-toxic. The cleanest fuel known to science is Hydrogen.

There is no Carbon. Therefore, no partially consumed hydrocarbons (PCH), no volatile organic compounds (VOC), no green house gasses CO_2, there's no NOx, or SOx, no particulates, no radiation, no Mercury. No ocean acidification. There are no pollutants at all. It's a water cycle.

Let's continue our inquiry, our "best fuel" would also need to be available to consumers distributed all over the earth. The resource, the basic feedstock needs to be available for as many people as possible to limit the wealth inequity which results from the restricted supplies for feedstock including oil wells, coal mines, strip mines, and fracking wells.

Let's sort our list of all fuels to find the most available feedstock. Sort. Top of the list: Hydrogen.

Hydrogen can be "produced" by adding electricity to water. This device, called an electrolyzer, separates the water molecule into its constituent elements, namely Oxygen and Hydrogen.

Since water covers over 70% of the earth, it is by far the most available energy feedstock on earth compared to any other resource. It's a water cycle where clean renewable electricity fed into water produces Hydrogen fuel. And, when the Hydrogen fuel is consumed you get high power, and most of the water back.

If you're keeping score that's three out of three for Hydrogen produced from renewable energy and water. But, let's continue. The next important criteria for defining the "best fuel" would be safety.

List all of our fuels, and their corresponding casualties, with the safest on top. Sort. Top of the list: Hydrogen.

As of this writing there are no deaths reported (to the author's knowledge) associated with any energy accidents in the Hydrogen industry even now a large industry in manufacturing going back decades. Not a one. How many people burn to death, or are badly injured in a car fire involving gasoline? Thousands each year. Gasoline is actually a dangerous liquid fuel. Carrying around tin cans full of gasoline under our cars is not safe. It's dangerous and thousands are killed or injured each year as a result.

Hydrogen as a fuel is the safest fuel by virtue of its characteristics. Hydrogen, first on the periodic table of elements is not only the most abundant material in the known universe, it's also the lightest. If it escapes, it's gone.

If there is ever a breech, it escapes fast, and up. At the speed of 6 stories a second, Hydrogen gas evaporates, if you will, and escapes into the atmosphere if given a path. Fossil fuel liquid fuels in contrast are heavier than air, and will soak around the fire and burn on the ground, and are notoriously dangerous.

Compared to all other fuels, Hydrogen is demonstrably safer handled properly. The Hydrogen industry in America and worldwide is already a mature industry working on industrial scale and has a long track record in the field for safety.

There we have it. Four top criteria for choosing the best fuel, and all of them come up with the same answer: Hydrogen. Science offers the ideal chemical fuel to use in the 21st century. It's the fuel which is clean, powerful, safe, and available to all people based on water. The fuel of the 21st century is Hydrogen. Solar produced hydrogen from water.

A Green New Deal recognizes science, and recognizes the market opportunities for evolving our exiting obsolete toxic fossil fuel paradigm with stronger, clean, available and safe renewably produced Hydrogen from water we see a major leap in our industrial technology.

A great leap is at hand, and its based on an industrial revolution. The industrial revolution of the 21st century, accelerated by the Green New Deal.

The Economics of Energy

We live in a world powered by fossil fuels. Energy is a commodity and has been from the beginning of our industrial age. The economics of energy is based on this fact. If you need energy, you must buy it from someone. Need it again? Buy it again.

Since John D. Rockefeller set this cast and business model the entire 20th century suffered from the economic inequity baked into the cake insuring the business model of Standard Oil was duplicated all over the world. Those who controlled the oil wells and sources of carbon controlled great wealth.

Militaries around the world made securing "holes in the ground" surrounded by men with guns the standard practice. This extreme "have" and "have-not" situation insured populations were confined to being indentured "energy consumers" where controlling petroleum and other Carbon feedstocks controlled all other aspects of economy. It's all about the money.

Control the physical means of production such as Oil as energy, then economies can be siphoned of money into those coffers who control the energy resources.

This is reality today. Imagine everyone's energy bill in aggregate. American energy consumers often pay an electric bill, a gasoline bill, a heating oil, and/or natural gas bill each month. Add all of these bills up and its more than health care and education. Energy is a commodity, and the total amount of money involved is staggering.

As a commodity, Energy both electricity and chemical fuels (i.e. gasoline, diesel, aviation fuels etc.) is big business.

American's pay the bill. And, because energy is vital to everything else, everyone pay's the bill or they can't run the machines vital in modern living.

A Green New Deal addresses the economics of energy and recognizes the "Commodity" nature of energy, as its been for three hundred years, is now facing a technology which obsoletes the commodity-based economics of energy all together.

A solar clean energy paradigm turns commodity into self-reliance, in essence, you produce your own energy onsite. All you need is the right gear.

Example. An average American home, as we've seen, typically has an electric bill, a natural gas, and/or heating oil bill, and a gasoline and/or diesel bill for fueling vehicles. Let's call it Electricity, Natural Gas, and Gasoline as an example.

In the new economy the house, (or other building) will have solar PV panels, either on the roof, or over the driveway, or on fence lines, or in any number of tasteful and functional forms on or near the house producing the home's essential primary energy. If a commercial or industrial building then rooftops, and parking lots are often large enough to deploy solar without using any new land. Equipped with batteries and power conditioning and solar thermal technology this home (building) power system is able to provide 100% of the energy consumption without a fuel bill.

Connection to an electrical grid is optional.

Since the home (building) already has an energy bill, the finance of the new system can be structured to be less than the current bill each month. In this way, the Green New Deal can produce a new energy system with immediate profit for the consumer, healthy returns for the underwriter, and an immediate win for energy stability, resilience and non-toxicity tackling a local problem and a global issue in one step.

In this example, renewable energy is the primary power converter onsite. The clean energy system provides the energy the house needs on demand. No loss of any lifestyle, and if designed properly provides greater performance. No one is living in a cave, they're living in a castle.

The energy systems of the 21st century are superior to fossil fuels. A Green New Deal is not a step backward in performance, its a step forward.

The point here is there are two economic models in play. The old commodity approach to energy, and the other a clean energy self-sufficient model based on fixed cost hardware.

Each economic approach requires hardware with one big difference: the fuel. Energy technology always requires some sort of gear. The difference is fuel costs, and toxic liability. Commodity based energy charges the consumer every time they consume the energy, a fuel cost. Need more energy? Pay more money. The solar clean energy system has no fuel costs therefore all costs are limited to hardware and maintenance, much lower in operating costs compared to buying fuel all the time.

Which system offers the greatest benefit to the consumer? To the average American? To the citizens of the world?

The clean energy system. By packaging hardware, and packaging finance, the actual cost per month paid by the consumer is lower using the solar system from the start.

The profit is immediate. Using clean energy systems the real cost of America's energy bill will go down. Why?

No fracking, no mining, no drilling, no tanker trucks, no pipelines, no fuel depots, no supertankers, no oil railroads or toxicity required. In the new economy carbon as a fuel is not involved.

Where do we put the solar panels?

Producing thousands of GWHs of energy from solar energy requires area for solar collection distributed at the loads. Solar photovoltaic (PV) panels can be deployed on rooftops across sectors. Next time you're on an airplane as you approach an airport look at all the empty space available on commercial rooftops.

The solar energy falling on typical warehouses is more than sufficient to power the building and in warmer locations solar panels on the roof reduce the heat-loading of the building. The power plants of the future will not be remote, they'll be as close as the parking lot. There is plenty of room if we think in dual use.

Solar panels can be deployed on walls, over walkways, and fences, on poles, on surfaces, there is a lot of flexibility on where they are placed, the point is there are many places to put them.

Providing shade from the sun and protection from rain and snow even covering roadways with solar canopies can provide multiple benefits and enormous amounts of power and energy throughout the day to power loads, charge batteries and produce hydrogen fuel from water.

The greatest opportunity in the urban setting is the parking lot.

It's always surprising to consider how much land area is devoted to parking. Over 30% of Houston within the city limits is devoted to parking. Parking lots, are the best kept secret in real estate. They're everywhere you want to be. Location, location, location.

Building solar canopies over parking lots provides pleasant cover from the elements, sun, rain and snow keeping the parking lot clear for safe travel in all weather conditions.

Parking lots exist in sufficient areas adjacent to the electrical loads and represents an enormous resource if partially covered with solar canopies.

Modern solar PV electric systems are solid state. There are no moving parts. Compare this to a coal-fired power plant using thousands of moving parts.

Imagine the long line of "stuff" required to mine the coal, load the coal, transport the coal over often hundreds if not thousands of mile, then off load the coal, and burn the coal spewing toxicity just to boil water.

Burning coal releases an increasing stream of toxins which linger in the environment and damage biology for centuries. Which world do we want to live in?

The parking lots are typically so large around Walmart Stores the collective solar energy which could be harvested from Walmart alone could power a large percentage of electric vehicles (EV) across the country.

Distributed energy resources such as solar powered charging stations, peaking stations, demand peak shaving, bulk base power production ranging from small to large loads can be powered onsite with solar PV as the primary power producer.

Parking lots covered with solar PV would provide in aggregate Gigawatt hours (GWH) of new energy with no new land required.

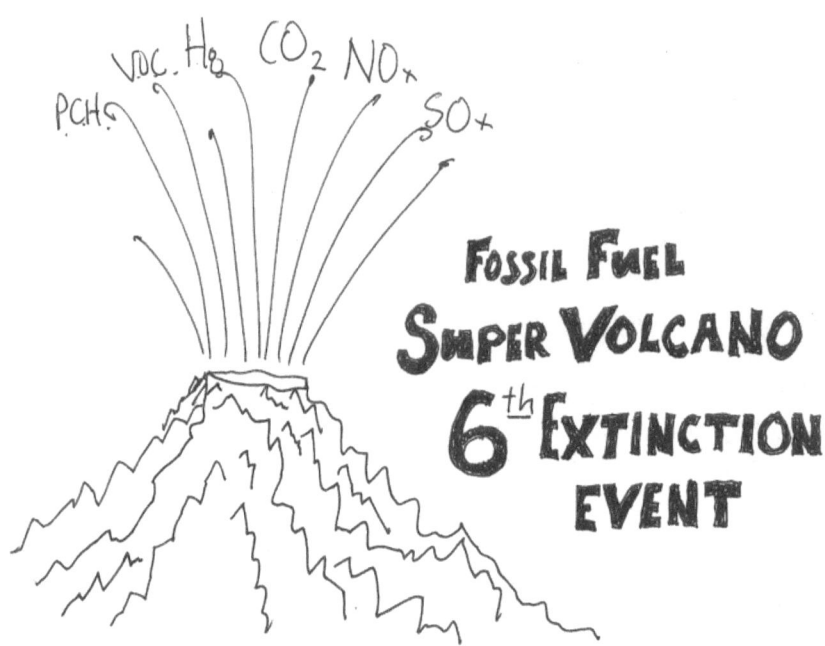

VOC. H_2 CO_2 NO_x
PCHs
SO_x

FOSSIL FUEL
SUPER VOLCANO
6th EXTINCTION
EVENT

Fossil Fuels

Imagine, our entire modern civilization is based on burning Carbon fuels often sourced across the globe requiring moving massive amounts of "stuff" everywhere and call it energy. We dig carbon out of the earth, we scrap, frack, drill and extract all of the carbon fuel we can reach.

It takes a lot of energy to do this. Next, we transport the carbon often thousands of miles by railroad, pipeline, supertanker, and any other means which also takes a lot of energy all the while adding costs.

Next, vast amounts of remotely sourced petroleum is delivered to refineries where it's cooked and fractioned into various distillates, i.e. gasoline, diesel, heating oil, kerosine, tar etc. This takes a lot of energy.

Next, the distillates are transported again from the refineries to the gasoline fueling stations distributed all over the country by pipeline then tanker trucks. This takes energy, and is adding cost.

At the end of the day, at last energy is available for sale. Of course, when used by the consumer then dumps enormous amounts of toxicity into the environment wasting 75% on average as waste heat and toxicity.

Just as the Automotive industry is dumping the need for oil all together going electric, the rest of the traditional fossil fuel markets will abandon this toxic and outdated approach to industrial energy.

The fallacy of this model is that carbon isn't needed at all, and we don't need to mine ancient sunlight. Carbon's just the stuff hydrogen is stuck to, the energy has always been, and always will be in the hydrogen, not the carbon.

Hydrocarbons are molecules formed exclusively from Hydrogen and Carbon. The energy, however, is in the hydrogen, not the carbon. Coal, a hydrocarbon which is mostly carbon and a little hydrogen has the lowest specific energy density (30 MJ/Kg).

Oil, has proportionally less carbon and more hydrogen and the energy density goes up (40 MJ/Kg). Natural gas, has even less carbon by proportion, and more hydrogen compared to oil and again the energy density goes still higher to (50 MJ/Kg).

Hydrogen, is a hydrocarbon with no carbon, and all hydrogen and has the highest specific energy density at (140 MJ/Kg). Industrial revolution has been defined by the energy content of our fuels. If the specific energy density doesn't go up, it's not evolution.

Energy in the 21st century

Our world is continuing to electrifying continuing a wave which begun with electrification starting in 1892. It's simply far easier to move electrons than to move molecules of stuff.

The fossil fuel industries dominance through the 18th, 19th, and 20th centuries, respectively, have reached the 21st century and have found their end.

There is only one way known to science able to provide distributed industrial scale energy to everyone on earth. There is only one solution which can provide the massive amounts of energy, and energy available for consumers is such quantity required to obsolete human poverty: the sun.

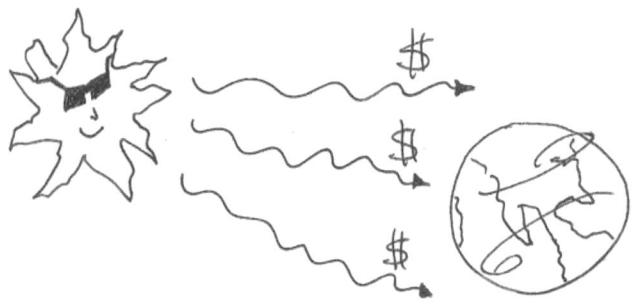

There is only one way to simultaneously solve climate disruption, acid rain, ocean acidification, species loss, habitat loss, DNA disruption, mercury poisoning, and all other toxic impacts of burning carbon: solar based industrial power.

There is only one way to provide the power, availability, safety, and non-toxicity using a fuel energy density far greater than used in the fossil fuel age: the sun.

There is only one way to produce energy in the quantities the future needs: solar electricity, and solar fuels produced locally.

The Green New Deal recognizes the only way forward capable of solving all our global problems is from clean energy.

Energy based on renewable sources, especially solar photovoltaics (although include any renewables available) provides the base electricity required to power our loads directly, store for future use, produce hydrogen fuel, and is non-toxic when used to not interfere with the essential biology of ourselves, and the natural world upon which we depend.

Chapter Five - Energy and Jobs

Industrial revolution always spurs massive job creation. We've seen the stimulus our recent digital revolutions have created with the rise of the tech companies. Jobs have been created where they never existed before. This is natural and important for economic health to keep the cutting edge of new industry formation. This happens as a result of industrial revolution. Solving problems creates jobs.

Energy, and job creation go hand in hand throughout history.

During the 1st industrial revolution, the use of coal rapidly replaced the sole reliance on human and animal muscle to do work. Even waterwheels were obsolete with rise of the new steam engine for base power. The energy paradigm changed, stimulating job creation in thousands of new factories rapidly growing the economy.

A massive transformation in jobs occurred as swarms of people migrated from rural jobs, to newly created urban jobs forcing people to live together in emerging cities. People living in such close quarter required political and social institutions to growth with them. The age of the factory was born, as well as mass consumption and mass markets. The economy took off, as well as social and political innovation.

Coal powered steam engines provided the power supply for heavy industry such as the steel industry, and railroads, further increasing the use of steam power for manufacturing, transportation, and all of the other activities of industry.

During the 2nd Industrial revolution, as Oil over Coal was unleashed with the internal combustion engine, electronics used for controlling mechanical machines increased. The number of people working on "information" surpassed the number of people working traditional labor, another impetus was given to the job market again as opportunity flourished and economies expanded. Industrial revolutions are good for job growth as entirely new categories of employment are created.

The rise of the "information age" part of the 2nd Industrial revolution (around 1920's) saw the processing of information, and applied to all sectors of economic activity, expanded the job market again. As more people worked beyond the production of goods and services, to include "information processing" and back office work required by larger markets being served, economic growth and labor markets grew with the logistics required to support them. As the 2nd Industrial Revolution flourished, so did job creation.

The 3rd Industrial Revolution occurred as Natural Gas and aviation fuels and the turbine engines which burned them converged. A new capability also emerging when optical systems controlled electronic systems, which in turn controlled mechanical systems. This industrial revolution taking hold in the 1950s and 1960s when information processing and signal control took on a new dimension ushering in the age of Optics with fiber optic communications, integrated circuits and advanced displays.

Again, energy and jobs skyrocketed in growth. Just as vacuum tubes used earlier in the century were obsolete with the introduction of solid state devices (Shockley 1954) and the rise of the "transistor," then the integrated circuit, and then quickly Very large Scale integrated circuits (VLIC), leading to the Optical Erasable Programmable Read Only Memory (OEPROM) chips and the subsequent computer advancements of the last decades expanded employment and job creation orders of magnitude.

All information age companies i.e. Google, Apple, Amazon to name a few are built on the historical evolution of science and technology. Entirely new markets are created and new jobs with them in each industrial revolution in turn.

As industrial revolutions evolve through the advancement of technology, job creation expands and economies grow. The past industrial revolutions leave us at the doorstep of yet another industrial revolution, the industrial revolution of the 21st century: the 4th Industrial Revolution. The revolution of sustainability. The industrial revolution for our future.

The 4th Industrial Revolution is outlined by the Green New Deal.

The forth industrial revolution stands on the shoulders of the previous three, and integrates renewable energy, energy storage, and energy dispatched from distributed resources with no toxicity or fuel costs, transforming the economy of fossil fuels into a sustainable, more powerful energy paradigm with no fuel costs or toxicity. An energy paradigm for the 21st century.

The Green New Deal is not about redistributing wealth, its about creating new wealth.

The greatest challenge and responsibility of our generation is to achieve a sustainable industrial society for future generations. An industrial society tapped into solar resources offers all people more energy, more choices, and more opportunity to pursue their happiness.

An industrial society with no toxicity, and unlimited access to freedom. Access to powerful non-toxic low cost energy is freedom.

With clean energy economies, use as much energy as you want. It won't hurt anyone, especially future generations. The major difference between fossil fuel based energy and a clean energy future: no toxicity, or fuel costs.

The Green New Deal is an industrial revolution which offers a real solution to local and global issues by recognizing a real solution must contain a commonality.

The Green New Deal recognizes there is a common solution to local and global issues. It's that commonality which makes this transition so powerful. It's comprehensive.

To stem the crisis of climate disruption, and the toxic poisoning of the environment American can lead all countries of the world in the rapid transition from fossil fuels to Solar clean fuels as the industrial standard.

America can save the world. We can lead the world the way we always have: through our example.

A Green New Deal is good for America because it positions America in a leadership position regarding the new energy paradigm based on industrial fuels from sunlight and water. If America leads, then we can provide these hardware and service solutions to the world America can export energy solutions with great economic returns.

If you don't have access to energy then you have no future. If you have access to energy, then there are no limits, the future is yours.

Job creation in the 21st century

Americans are suffering the pains of transition in many sectors facing forces such as automation, robotics, artificial intelligence and the pressures of internet based business which requires far fewer people than traditional brick and mortar retail we've known for two hundred years, all combine requiring many labor markets to transition.

A Green New Deal recognizes the transitional stresses the job market faces in light of the digital age and the convergence of dozens of industrial revolutions in progress across all sectors of the economy.

Chapter Six - Do you have an Electric Bill?

"It's much easier to fool someone, than to convince someone they're being fooled."

- Mark Twain -

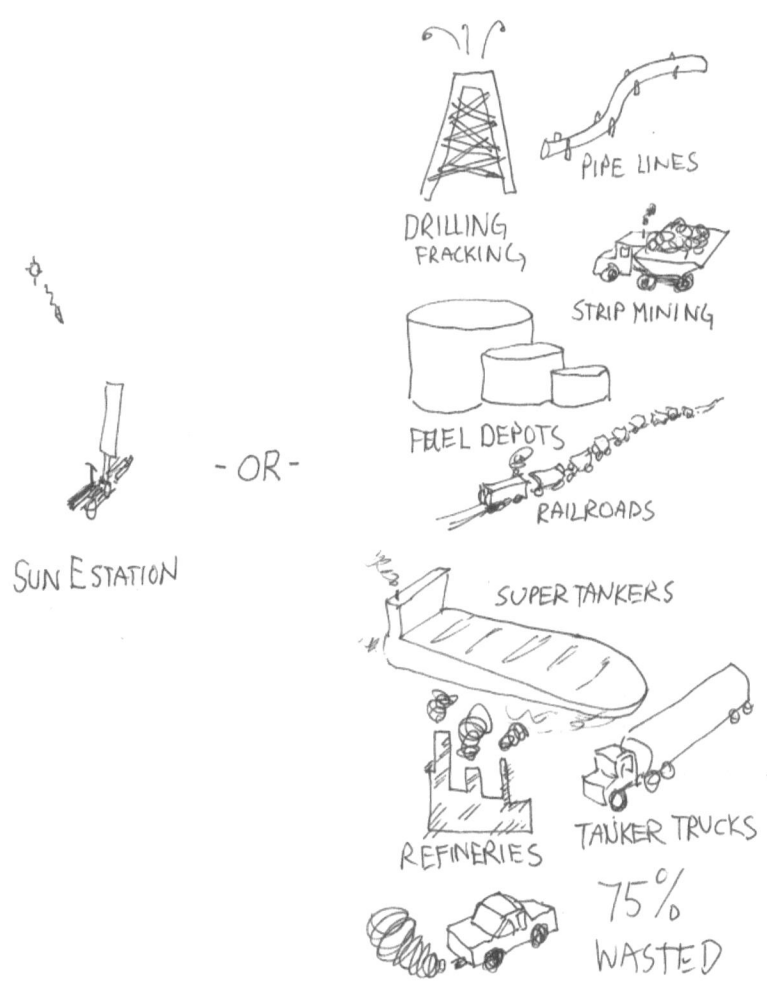

One of the biggest propaganda points of the opposition to a Green New Deal is the claim "... it will cost trillions!"

At best a half-truth, and therefore no truth, as it ignores the equally important question, "how much does it make?"

Do you have an electric bill? Almost certainly, and all of your neighbors too. After all, electricity is a "business." Since we need the electricity, we pay the bill.

Imagine everyone's electric bill within one mile of you. Add them all up, is it a lot of money? Sure it is, and this goes to the next big lie of the fossil fuel interests regarding anything other than them: "It will cost trillions!"

The fact is, globally we already pay trillions. The Energy industry is absolutely huge. Americans alone have a combined energy bill (electric and chemical fuels) exceeding $100 billion per Month!

Energy is the biggest business on Earth. It's the life blood of modern industry. However, energy doesn't mean just fossil fuels as the industry wants you to believe, energy means energy from any source.

At the moment we buy energy worldwide largely from fossil fuel companies which siphon off hundreds of billions of dollars per month from the world economies. Must it always be so?

If we didn't have fuel costs, could we use those funds for other purposes?

We use energy both as electricity, and chemical fuels i.e. gasoline, aviation fuel, diesel. Combined the energy industry siphons over 15% of the world economy away under the guise of "fuel costs." The game they play is "hey, you need us."

A Green New Deal challenges this paradigm by using an energy technology which has no fuel costs. Under fossil fuels, America and the world pays a collective electric and fossil fuel bill of trillions of dollars annually.

Under a Green New Deal, America's collective energy bill will go down, and continue to go down as more and more Solar PV and solar clean fuel systems come online displacing toxic expensive and unreliable fossil fuels. If structured properly the Green New Deal will happen at a profit. A profit to Americans in greater health, lower real energy costs, and expanded opportunity to generate hard currency onsite where it is used promoting distributed capitalism and individual freedom.

The reality is there is more than enough money to provide universal health care, universal public tuition, and universal opportunity for economic development, it's currently being spent on fossil fuels. Diverting these enormous revenues away from fossil fuel companies and back into the public's hands will provide real economic stimulus. People can spend the money on living, not down a hole only enslaved to pay it again, and again. Free the money, and you free the people.

The sustainable economic growth induced by a Green New Deal would invigorate every level of employment, and expand real economic opportunities for all sectors and segments of our American society by lowering real costs. "A penny saved, is a penny earned," Franklin said. True then, and true now.

Another big lies told by the fossil fuel industry. "You need us," they say, "you need fossil fuels,... or,... you'll end up living in caves."

The fossil fuel, and traditional electric utility industry is not too keen on renewables in general, and particularly if they change the market away from them, which they are. Therefore, they resist the truth of the matter as it's a scenario which sees them extinct much sooner than they think even possible to consider. This is the nature of industrial evolution. Step, step, leap.

Because the fossil fuel companies enjoy massive profits and enormous cash-flow syphoning off America's cash under the flag of fuel costs to the tune of hundreds of billions of dollars each year - they don't want to change.

Therefore, we hear disinformation such as "CO_2 is not a pollutant," or "They want the Government to control industries," or, "This will cost Trillions," or "Solar energy is Socialism" is just nonsense.

Solar energy is capitalism. Tapping into the industrial sun is in every energy consumer's self interest and prosperity.

Solar electricity and solar fuels is disruptive capitalism because it usurps an existing market (fossil fuels) which is siphoning trillions of dollars each year out of global economies, and with distributed capitalism opens up a new global participation. Clean energy is not controlled solely by access to holes in the ground surrounded by men with guns. Energy is now about access to the sky, and the natural energy around us amply available in any quantity you wish to harvest.

The future for Solar Hydrogen and a modern clean energy system is to take increasing market share from current fossil fuel markets and replace them with non-toxic and greater performance with new technology lowering real costs for consumers onsite. Consumers will benefit most from the Green New Deal and this is the heart of the effort, and why it will succeed. Evolving into a better way of powering this world over fossil fuels will generate sustainable growth of our economy for many decades to come.

Does the Government have an electric bill? Of course, and it's a whopper.

Add all of the Government building electric bills for any given state together and it's a big number. How many hundreds of Government buildings exist in each state? Thousands? The collective electric bill for Government buildings, including schools, public works, government agencies, on and on, all together add to a big bill. Add the government's fuel costs and you have a really large number.

This is the fiscal power of the Government used by not raising taxes, but by lowering costs. Either way approach can get a job done, but one is much less painful than the other.

Another example of the power of the Government's purchase power.

The largest user and consumer of Diesel fuel in the world is the US NAVY. Long a pioneer in seeking a way to reduce dependence on Diesel fuel, which the NAVY considers a national security risk, is an excellent place to start in the industrial transition to clean energy.

If the NAVY took its existing Diesel bill (how many hundreds of millions of dollars per year?) and began transitioning to Solar Hydrogen as fuel then energy security would increase as each NAVY base can produce its own Hydrogen fuel onsite at each base. This lowers the risk of fuel delivery interruption which is a major security risk during a time of conflict, not to mention ongoing costs.

A Green New Deal recognizes energy is fundamental. The 21st century will not run on the fuels of the 18th, 19th, and 20th centuries. Technology evolves and leaps, and we must use the best of it to solve real problems. Problems felt by each American, and our collective problems we face as a global species.

The one thing we can do which will help all aspects of our industrial civilization is to solve the energy paradigm. Turning toxic commodities, into non-toxic self-reliance.

A Green New Deal leads this charge.

Transportation has always been the hotbed of Industrial Revolution.

The 5 revolutions emerging now in Transportation

The rise of loading and unloading robots and Autonomous Vehicles, are putting increasing pressure on traditional transportation industry jobs. In America over three million truckers are facing their jobs being displaced by automation in the 2020s. As the autonomous vehicle capability comes on line the economics and the people required will change.

The Green New Deal recognizes these technological trends and realizes the future of transportation is extremely bright if anticipated and employees properly prepared. The market for transportation is massive, and in transition. America leading this transportation revolution has most to gain.

A Green New Deal recognizes the opportunity to unleash a new generation of transportation options, and to build new infrastructure creating new jobs and new categories of jobs. These new jobs to be filled by the changing work force.

A Green New Deal understands there are no less than five (5) industrial revolutions now occurring in the transportation industry. The convergence of five new waves.

Revolution one: The rise of the EV

Electric vehicles (EV) are one of the game changers in today's transportation market. Why? EVs offer higher performance and value for the consumer than internal combustion engines (ICE) which have dominated the automobile market for over a century.

Traditional piston engines have over 2,000 moving parts. EVs have about 20. This basic fact makes an electric drive train much superior to an old fashioned explosion piston internal combustion engine (ICE) dating back in basic design 150 years.

Modern EVs are simply better cars by any metric you wish to cite. Performance? EVs can deliver instant full torque to the drive train.

A piston engine takes time to power up when you accelerate. The EV power performance is vastly superior to any piston engine inherently. EV drag racers beat chemical liquid fuel racers by delivering instant torque to the wheels. Electricity moves nearly instantly. In contrast, mechanical drive trains take time to transfer power through mechanical linkage. EVs are more powerful by delivering that power instantly on demand.

Pollution? Internal combustion engines are not terribly efficient, typically much less than 22% in the field. Which means most of the effort made to drill, scrap, frack, and mine, process, transport and distribute fossil fuels is wasted out the tailpipe over 75% of the energy ejected as toxins and waste heat. Why go to so much trouble to attain fossil fuels, only to waste most of it out the tailpipe, and with such toxicity no less?

It only makes sense if you're selling it.

Burning fossil fuels produces nearly 20 lb. of air pollution for each gallon of gasoline burned. Multiply this by billions of gallons of fuel burned worldwide each day and it means we are pouring on the order of tens of millions of tons of air pollution into our environment each Day!

It's hard to visualize how much stuff we're pumping into the atmosphere and oceans to try to absorb. Fossil fuels are toxic, and this goes to our point. The exhaust from piston engines are toxic. Piston engines waste nearly three quarters of the energy in the fuel when they burn it out of the exhaust pipe. Burning fossil fuels is 75% inefficient. How is that a good idea to run an industrial world? It's not.

An Electric Vehicle (EV) is only as clean as the source of electricity charging it. Plug an EV into your electrical grid and the toxicity of the energy is a function of the utility charging the EV. Dirty utility, dirty electricity.

If you charge your EV with solar photovoltaics (solar electricity) then you're not only zero emission, you're zero-emission from soup to nuts. The entire energy life cycle is clean. Why? Because there is no Carbon involved as a fuel, there is no pollution in operating the vehicle.

The electric drive train of a modern EV obsoletes a mechanical piston engine hands down as superior in doing work as the early cars over the horse. This is why EV will ultimately win market share and the decade of the 2020s will see the end of piston engines used in transportation. By the end of the 2020s not one major manufacturer of automobiles will produce a piston engine. It went the way of the buggy whip.

The 2nd Revolution in Transportation

Hydrogen. As we've seen above, by every major metric: power, non-toxicity, availability, and safety, respectively, the fuel of the 21st century is Hydrogen sourced from renewable energy and water.

There has been a debate about EVs being all battery using Lithium ion batteries, for example, verses using Fuel Cells using Hydrogen producing water as the only waste product to power cars.

In some ways this is a false debate. Both are EVs. An EV is traditionally thought of as an "all battery" vehicle. The fuel cell vehicle we'll call FCEV still uses an electric drive train. Both are electric vehicles. The fuel cell makes the electric vehicle hydrogen assisted.

A FCEV vehicle still uses an electric battery, but the battery is much smaller, only 5% of capacity compared to an all battery EV.

Therefore, a Fuel Cell assisted EV can penetrate the market despite limits to battery production by using far less battery material. Using a battery only 5% of an all battery EV means 20 times more market share can be achieved for a given amount of battery production. The introduction of Fuel Cell assisted Electric cars will thrust the "EV" market from single digit to dominance in market share for new cars sold.

The smaller battery in an fuel cell EV is used for instant response and transitions, but the heavy lifting is done by the fuel cell. The fuel cell is an engine which operates at three times the efficiency of a typical piston engine. It's more powerful, and has nearly no moving parts, and fueled with hydrogen and oxygen from the air entirely non-toxic.

The debate between an all battery EV, or fuel cell assisted EV, will be decided in the marketplace. America's love of SUVs and Trucks is best served by Fuel Cell assisted EV.

The problem is not the car (SUV), it's the fuel. Hydrogen fuel cells are ideal for SUVs and Trucks where you need power and safety. Given the market appeal of SUVs and Trucks hydrogen fuel cell power makes the choice clear. Electric batteries are fine for smaller loads, but heavy loads, trucks, railroads, construction equipment, farm equipment etc. these larger loads can't be easily battery operated with Lithium ion cells. Fuel cells, however, are perfectly suited to these large loads. It's a fuel cell future.

The 3rd Revolution in Transportation

Ride share. Ride share service companies including but not limited to Uber, and Lyft have had a dramatic impact on the nature of the labor market in personal transportation. First on cab drivers and traditional transportation employees, now rapidly impacting entire industries including adding to the obsolescence of car dealerships everywhere. Perhaps most significant is the emerging trend for younger generations to feel no real need to ever buy a car in the first place.

The 21st century is about access verses owning. For personal transportation the need for owning the vehicle is disappearing. Ride share companies offer the traveling public an alternative to all of the risk, and monthly expense owning a traditional car presents.

Owning a car requires, typically, a monthly car payment, an insurance payment, maintenance costs, repair costs exposure, and of course fuel costs. Add these all up and it takes a lot of time to earn the money each month to have personal transportation: to own a car.

Ride share companies say, pay as you go. If you need it, or want it we're here. Don't use us? Then, enjoy no costs. For many younger people with college debt, high living costs, and other expenses as a reality of American life the option of not owning a car can save thousands per year, lower stress, and increase eMobility options.

Ride share comes with another revolutionary influence moving into the mix: the autonomous car. As autonomous cars expand public options for personal travel additional pressure on traditional jobs in transportation including bus drivers, train operators and public transit may see downward pressure on revenues as the traveling public enjoys more options and multi modal access to new options for travel.

The 4th revolution in Transportation

Personal Mobility Devices (PMDs). A new category of personal transportation has emerged which will impact the century old transit option of trains, planes and automobiles and it's the Personal Mobility Device (PMD). Electric Vehicles (EV) are not just cars anymore.

EVs now include eScooters, eBikes, eMopeds, eMotorcycles, eWheelchairs, eGolf carts and other electric conveyances rapidly emerging as a new set of options for public travel especially the ride share market. Why own, when you can access?

Consider a transportation market such as Vietnam. Many citizens of Vietnam travel by small engine Mopeds. Streets often clogged with swarms of little scooters belching blue smoke, dripping oil, and always that high pitched whining of the piston engines. Most of the world travels this way.

Imagine the impact of widely distributed stand-alone Solar Charging Stations on transportation in Vietnam and beyond.

When you park an eScooter, eBike or eMoped, you dock at a solar powered Sun eStation™ and the Personal Mobility Device (PMD) begins charging.

The Sun eStation™ uses solar energy, (and onboard batteries) to power the eMobility devices providing charging when the vehicle (eScooter/eBike etc.) is docked.

Build enough distributed Sun eStations™ and an entire transportation paradigm can shift as quickly as smart phones outdated land lines.

In one few swoop, an entirely new technology, distributed solar charging stations, offer the traveling public no fuel costs, and no toxicity in personal travel and a new dimension in ride share - solar powered transportation.

Distributed solar powered charging stations will change people's lives in transportation as profoundly as Smart phone technology changed our lives in communications over the landline.

Public transit systems can either compete with these new options, or they can embrace them, and get in front of the wave. For over a century buses and trains have dominated public transit.

If public transit expanded the modes of transportation options by including their own multi modal ride share programs offering eBikes, eScooters, and other EVs, then the public revenues would increases as the public uses these easy access modes of travel.

Clean energy infrastructure for the 21st century is the key. The electrification of the transportation system is inevitable.

The Green New Deal recognizes this evolution and increase in efficiency with solar clean energy as the primary power producers distributed throughout services ares we see the emergence of a new kind of energy - local solar power companies.

Today, the electric utilities and petroleum product producers are all based on a tightly controlled Centralized model of supply, processing and distribution of energy.

This business model was designed over a century ago.

For electric utilities the model has been large remote power plants, typically burning coal, far away from the service area to conceal the massive pollution streams, then use long high power transmission lines to bring the electricity back to the service area where it is stepped down, distributed and sold.

This old Centralized model of electricity production is rendered obsolete in the 21st century.

THE OLD UTILITY

TOXIC

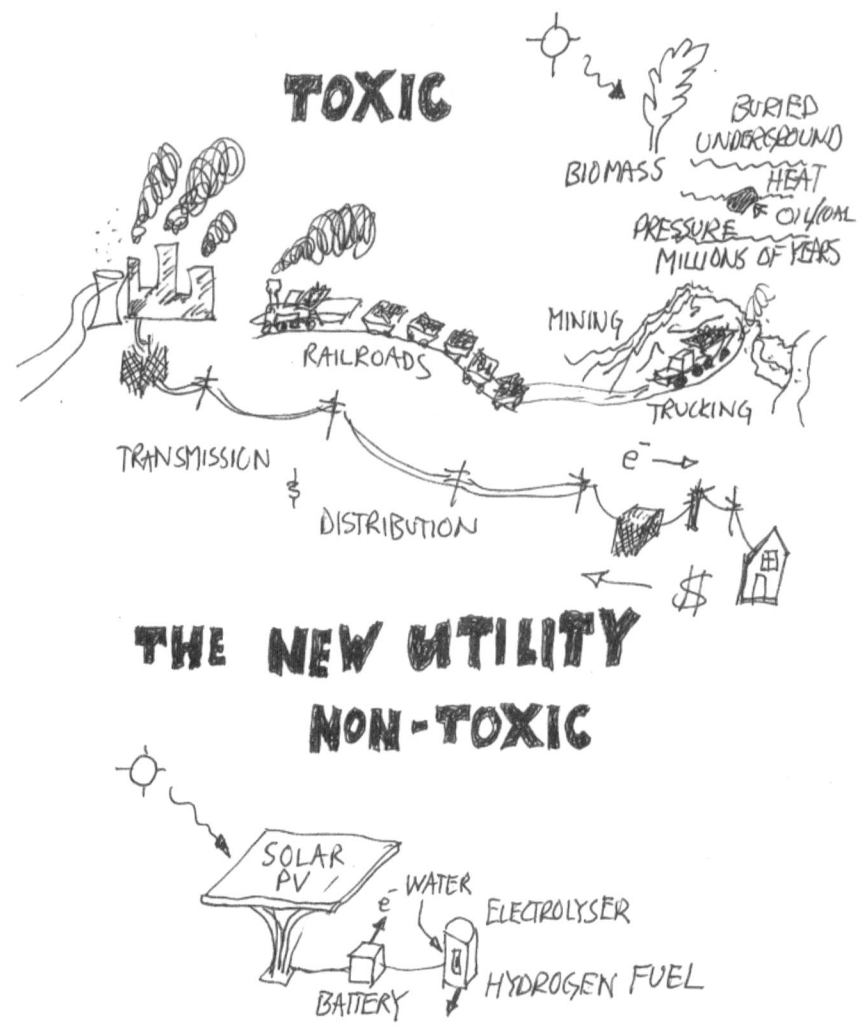

BIOMASS

BURIED UNDERGROUND
HEAT
PRESSURE OIL/COAL
MILLIONS OF YEARS

MINING

RAILROADS

TRUCKING

TRANSMISSION

DISTRIBUTION

e^- →

$

THE NEW UTILITY
NON-TOXIC

SOLAR PV

e^- WATER ELECTROLYSER

BATTERY

HYDROGEN FUEL

Power plants of the 21st century will be distributed, not centralized.

These distributed resources (DR) are organized in micro-grids which can share energy or disconnect from each other increasing resilience during an emergency. Instead of three major grids powering the United States increasingly vulnerable to disruption (the bad kind), the new grid will be a distributed network of stand-alone micro-grids which can work together or separately.

Micro grids powered by solar energy, or other renewables, using storage with smart grid technology can feed into a larger grid on demand by the system operator (SO), or used to power the local loads, or both.

This Distributed Utility (DU) model is understood by the Green New Deal as the shape of the future and a pathway to benefit the American citizen, and energy consumer with reliable, low cost, non-toxic, resilient and accessible energy for any use: transportation, home power, commercial power, and industrial power.

Planning, building, and operating this new energy paradigm will stimulate job creation and make up for jobs displaced by the shrinking fossil fuel industry, and other jobs displaced by automation, artificial intelligence, and other digital revolutions, and assists in training and placement in the high growth industries of clean energy.

The new economy based on clean energy will be the economic engine for growth not just for a few years but for decades to come.

A sustainable growth, which doesn't throw future generations under the toxic bus.

The 5th Revolution in Transportation

21st century clean energy infrastructure and innovation.

New ways of travel. Innovation is the life spirit of an economy wishing to grow.

From innovation, benefits continue to increase for Americans, and all people who embrace real advances.

Trains, planes, and automobiles is a popular phrase to explain what we've all used for transportation for over a century. However, new technologies have opened up not only improvements such as high speed rail, but many entirely new modes of travel.

Whether traveling under the ground, through the water, below the water, on the surface, or through the air, technologies and industrial creativity open up cleaver ways of moving people and cargo.

Consider the entrance of drones delivering packages. In Africa, such delivery systems drop essential medicines to remote villages when no other means existed, and has saved lives. Some of those villages don't have electricity, yet the 21st century brings in a new technology and lives are changed in an instant.

The next step is to solar power the drones with solar charging stations. And, the villages themselves. Demonstrations of new modes and methods of delivering cargo and people are expanding in market share and will soon be a major player in the multi billion dollar business of delivery reaching every corner of the globe.

The Green New Deal embraces these advancements and encourages their development.

The economics of transportation is changing.

For over a century, other than public transportation the focus was owning your own car or truck. Since we first fell in love with cars over a 150 years ago, including the entire 20th century, and the beginning of the 21st century owning your own transportation was the norm.

Today, this paradigm is changing rapidly as Ride Share has opened Pandora's Box unleashing not only a ride share for cars, but is now expanding rapidly into personal mobility devices (i.e. eScooters, eBikes, eMopeds, eMotorcycles, eWheelchairs, eGolf Carts), even private jets have entered this new "shared" economy.

Instead of owning a car. Many travelers, long used to cabs and rental car options, are going with the Uber/Lift model where you only pay per trip. You don't own the car. You don't need to.

You don't pay a monthly car payment (usually the second largest debt item of the American citizen), you don't pay a monthly insurance bill, you don't pay maintenance or repair bills. And, you don't pay for fuel. You only pay for the ride. This new economic model for transportation is growing rapidly because it brings value to the consumer.

New technology, opens new markets, as new companies (and existing companies) expand to meet the new market opportunity resulting in economic growth. This is the heart beat of the Green New Deal.

Economics of Commodity based Energy

The big industrial secret is "you have to pay someone for energy," and "you have to pollute the earth to attain a modern life style."

Both of these deceptions hides the plain truth: if you add up everyone's electric and energy bill, it's more than the cost of healthcare and education combined. We already have the money. We're just spending it on fossil fuels.

In other words, to fund healthcare and education unleashing human potential as never seen before, all of the money needed is already in your pocket now - spent on fuel. We're just paying it all out to energy companies. Trillions of dollars per year.

Is there a better way? Yes, the Green New Deal.

Clean energy with no fuel costs, changes the economics of energy in favor of the consumers: less costs and toxic liabilities means more money in people's pockets: a lot more. Add up your electric, gasoline, fuel oil, and natural gas bills in aggregate. Over one year how much do you pay for fuel?

Can we imagine the worldwide economic stimulus resulting from freeing this enormous amount of capital once used for fuel costs? In America alone we pay over $100 billion per month for energy (electricity, gasoline, diesel, aviation fuel, etc.).

The transition to a solar economy means the influx of trillions of dollars into the world economy annually, formally paid as fuel costs, available to help fund the health and economic prosperity to "promote the general welfare" and allow our citizens to reap the benefits of this new energy paradigm.

Wealth created everywhere by tapping into the hard currency of solar produced electricity enables people to tap into this enormous and already distributed industrial strength power supply: the sun.

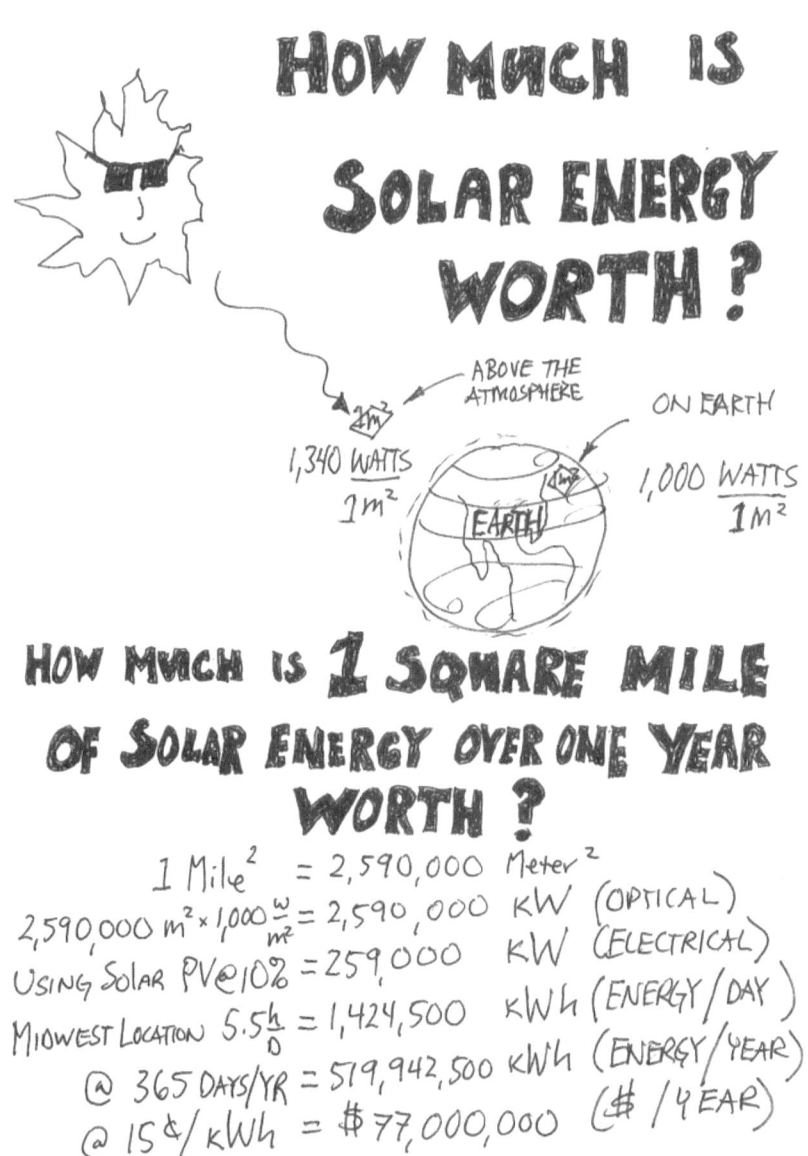

HOW MUCH IS SOLAR ENERGY WORTH?

ABOVE THE ATMOSPHERE

ON EARTH

$$\frac{1,340 \text{ WATTS}}{1 m^2}$$

EARTH

$$\frac{1,000 \text{ WATTS}}{1 m^2}$$

HOW MUCH IS 1 SQUARE MILE OF SOLAR ENERGY OVER ONE YEAR WORTH?

$$1 \text{ Mile}^2 = 2,590,000 \text{ Meter}^2$$

$$2,590,000 \text{ m}^2 \times 1,000 \tfrac{w}{m^2} = 2,590,000 \text{ KW (OPTICAL)}$$

$$\text{USING SOLAR PV@10\%} = 259,000 \text{ KW (ELECTRICAL)}$$

$$\text{MIDWEST LOCATION } 5.5 \tfrac{h}{D} = 1,424,500 \text{ kWh (ENERGY/DAY)}$$

$$@ 365 \text{ DAYS/YR} = 519,942,500 \text{ kWh (ENERGY/YEAR)}$$

$$@ 15 ¢/kWh = \$77,000,000 \text{ (\$ /YEAR)}$$

Business Example:

Consider the energy costs of a small business, say a Caterer.

The kitchen has ovens so we have, typically, a Natural Gas bill, and of course an electric bill. With a delivery truck we also have a gasoline bill. Let's put the kitchen energy costs at $500 per month, and the gasoline bill of $500 per month for an example. The energy bill each month for this business owner under these assumptions is $1,000 per month.

Since energy is vital, the bill gets paid. Let's make a five year plan (as best we can as we don't know the future cost of fossil fuel energy). At $1,000 per month the business owner will spend $12,000 per year, and over 5 years $60,000 in energy cost at constant prices.

Of course, not knowing the future cost of energy, this assumes no increase in fuel prices over 5 years. The ten years of fossil fuels will cost at least $120,000 out of pocket. After 10 years, of course you just keep paying if you need energy, which of course you do, and will under the fossil fuel commodity based energy world.

How can a solar energy system be installed and lower costs in real time?

The answer is Equipment Lease Financing.

Most americans lease their new cars using equipment lease finance. When you buy a new car you don't typically walk in with a suitcase full of money, instead you pay $399 per month.

Under an equipment lease finance package, an underwriter buys the car in your stead, and holds title to the car (asset) while they lease it to the lessee (you) for a schedule of monthly payments, and for a given length time (term).

The underwriter earns profit because the incoming lease payments pay off the principle and include interest. The Lessee likes the deal because they didn't need to come up with all the capital upfront to get the car.

The dealership likes the deal because they earn a commission. The manufacturer likes the deal because they receive a paid order. As long as the bills are paid on time by the Lessee, everyone gets what they want.

Back to our example of the business owner with the $1,000 monthly energy bill. Using the equipment lease finance structure a solar energy company packages the hardware, and maintenance, such that the monthly lease payment is substantially less than the amount the owner currently pays for energy.

Structuring the monthly payment to be less than the current bill a solar energy system can be installed with a payment of $750 per month, for example. Adjusting the term of the lease will adjust the payment amounts until the right balance is found.

Under this financial structure example, the owner sees a real reduction of monthly energy costs (25% less) starting the first month.

The money formerly paid for fuel costs, have been redirected to pay down solar hardware. After the term of the lease, the equipment is entirely depreciated and with solar PV panels typically offering a 30 year warranty, with typical lease terms ranging from 3 to 7 years - there are decades of clean energy production ahead.

The business owner has a lower monthly bill saving 25% during the first lease package. Over the first five years the Lessee saved $15,000 paying $45,000 instead of the fossil fuel $60,000. Fifteen thousand dollars now freed for other uses including healthcare, and educational costs or expanding the business.

After 5 years and the lease completed, a planned upgrade is performed on the hardware and a new lease packaged issued at a much lower rate again.

The second five year lease package drops the lease payment another 25% (equipment has already been paid down in the first lease) to $500 per month. During the second 5 year lease package the business owner is paying 50% less than the original fossil fuel monthly bill which they surely would otherwise be paying.

After ten years, under fossil fuels the owner would expect to pay a minimum of $120,000. Using the solar equipment lease package the savings over the first five years is $15,000, and over the second term (50% less) saves $30,000. Total savings (real profit) to the consumer over ten years using leasing over fuel costs is $45,000.

Do we think a $45,000 less expense on energy costs would help this small business owner?

All of this by free market means. Free market mechanisms we use in our economy all the time.

Using this method there are no added taxes, no rebates or incentives. Using those tools would only accelerate the transition, however on its own value equipment lease financing could achieve a global transition because it generates profit.

Capitalism at its best.

A solar clean energy economy uses capitalism to solve problems, and generate profit for all energy consumers. Including future generations.

This is the economic stimulus of the Green New Deal.

Chapter Seven - Opposition to Change

"People go through three reactions when hearing a revolutionary idea: the first reaction is "Oh, that will never work," then it becomes, "Well, ok, it will work, but why would you want to?, to then become "See, I always told you it was a good idea!"

- Arthur C. Clarke -

As the story has been for centuries there is change, and opposition to change.

Throughout the ages technology has evolved, and as technology evolved we've seen social change soon follow. Often with great sacrifice, the modern age has seen more social and economic benefits than generations before as each industrial revolution unleashes new freedoms and frontiers.

From our beginnings in the stone age, technology has always impacted human civilization.

From the stone age we arrived at the Copper age a revolutionary leap in human capabilities.

As we developed, we then produced Bronze from Copper by adding a little Tin, and our entire collective of Western and Eastern cultures, empires, and dynasties were thrust into the increasing capability of man unstoppable in its momentum. Technology was accelerating, and so were we.

From the Bronze age we leaped into the Iron Age with hotter furnaces where now common ores, instead of relatively rare tin, could be forged in mass quantities into tools, farm implements, larger machines, and of course superior weapons for conquest.

After the fall of Rome, it took centuries for Western Europe to wake from the dark ages as history soon hurled us through the Renaissance, into the Age of Reason, and finally into the Industrial Age unleashing a new technological man hurling again towards the future in leaps and bounds unimagined.

Throughout all of these major transitions, there is always opposition by those who hope the world will stay the way it was. In reality, the world never stays the same.

History shows industrial revolution after industrial revolution. Once separated by thousands of years, then centuries, then years, and months, industrial revolution in the modern age is almost a daily event.

Even a few decades ago the idea of a hand-held "smartphone" super computers networked into a world wide web used by almost everyone was unimaginable by most "experts" in the field only a few decades ago.

So it is now, it has always been, when people advance, there is opposition until they themselves make use of the new technology.

Opponents to the Green New Deal will often attempt fear mongering and old fashioned name calling to promote fear and deception to protect the big industrial lie, that all people must pay them for energy. Fortunately, the lie is exposed, and the technology exists which obsolete the hydrocarbon man soon to be relegated to a chapter in history.

A solar energy based industrial society promotes Capitalism more than anything. It promotes capitalism because it brings a new power supply to everyone who has an existing energy bill. Once people have lower costs, and a ready supply of electricity people get busy on improving their lives, and their neighbor's lives by starting new businesses, expanding existing ones. Prosperity on a grand scale founded on self-sufficiency and self-determination.

The Green New Deal understands the heart of capitalism worldwide is to empower people on an individual and local level at the most fundamental level: energy. What's more empowering than a stand alone solar power system with no fuel costs?

Self-reliance, independence, self-determination, and capitalism will all be enhanced with the power of distributed energy. Energy independence, is real independence.

Fossil fuel interests are not new to the game of hiding the real truth about energy: we don't need Carbon, and we don't need to pollute.

Long in the tooth, the fossil fuel interests have worked tirelessly to influence and dumb down the public understanding of science and technology to always bolster the deception that we need to burn Carbon.

Universities, and media institutions funded by petrodollars has groomed and denuded the public debate to distract, disinform, and discourage clean energy development. Take the example of the beloved PBS show "NOVA." From the opening credits we see the major "donor" or sponsor of NOVA is David Koch a large fossil fuel industrialist. NOVA announcing "Promoting american's understand of science." Really? America's understanding, or misunderstanding of science?

How many shows are produced about clean energy? A few. How many shows produced about climate disruption? A few, with little attention to solutions. How many NOVA episodes produced decrying fossil fuel pollution and toxicity? A few. How many produced about solar hydrogen fuels and a sustainable hydrogen economy? None, to the author's knowledge, or nearly no mention.

The fossil fuel propaganda machine has been in high gear to support anything which doesn't threaten market share. Including dominating (Koch's name is largest and first) pubic broadcasting to keep the lid nailed shut all around. Keep the world addicted to fossil fuels. Suppress the information for real solutions, and a "business as usual" world will continue.

The absence of Solar hydrogen fuels from the curriculum in our schools, colleges, universities and media programs is not an accident. It's done deliberately to dumb down the understanding and discussion of clean energy fuels. After all they have their business interests to protect.

However, industrial revolution can't be contained. Transportation and base load power generation is in transition. The writing is already on the wall.

Is the Automobile Industry abandoning Oil?

For over a hundred years there has been a tight symbiosis between the Oil and Automotive industries. For over a century the Oil industry supplied the liquid fossil fuels burned in almost all cars, trucks, vessels, aircraft, and jets. While the oil industry produced and sold the liquid fuels, the automobile industry produced and sold the cars in which they burned. Hand, in glove.

A deep, mutually dependent symbiotic relationship formed over a century between building cars and trucks, and filling them with Rock oil distillates.

However, over the last decade a new player has emerged in the automotive industry with dramatic implications for both the fossil fuel and automotive industries: the electric vehicle (EV).

The automotive industry has embraced the EV with billions of dollars of annual worldwide investment. All major automotive manufacturers all over the world have pushed all their chips in - the future of cars is electric.

The oil industry, in contrast has simply done nothing. Does the automotive industry know something the oil industry doesn't?

Married for a hundred years is there a divorce in the wind?

In the early 1990s, GM launched the EV1 early electric car and offered a basic electric vehicle which can be charged at home, and sometimes at work.

Although limited in range by today's standards, the EV1 proved extremely popular with drivers. Quiet, powerful, with no need of a gas station, and now with extended range, the EV is not produced by just a few automobile makers, they're manufactured by every major car manufacturer worldwide. Something significant has changed in the transportation industry.

The piston engine is once again facing its obsolescence.

Just as the jet engine obsoleted piston engines in most commercial and military aircraft after WWII, the EV will obsolete piston engines in cars and trucks.

Piston engines become obsolete for the same reasons any technology becomes obsolete, the new electric power-train is simply better.

Greater performance and benefits for the driver, proves the formula to winning market share.

EV market share at the time of this writing is growing 85% annually worldwide, and although about 1% of new car sales worldwide, the world of the EV is upon us as market share will accelerate each year.

If EV growth in market share continues at 85% annually starting at 1%, it will only take 8 years to achieve 100% market share. The decade of the 2020s will change everything in the automotive market as all vehicles are going electric.

What about the oil companies?

Oil is sold worldwide for many applications but most of the market is transportation fuels to the tune of billions of dollars per week.

Aren't the oil companies concerned about the EV, after all they don't use gas stations? Sure they are, but their only play is to continue their deception, keep the company line, and hope the automotive companies come to their senses.

Well, the automobile companies have come to their senses knowing any Auto manufacturer without an EV to offer will be left in the dust.

One decade after GM abandoned their EV1 offering, the company went bankrupt requiring public assistance to get operational again.

Is it a coincidence GM went bankrupt by miss reading their own customers and historical trends? GM went the way of Kodak and Polaroid.

Only with bankruptcy, and government bailouts did GM reemerge having lost the leading edge when they abandoned with EV1. GM didn't understand the impact of disruptive technology: electric over explosion internal combustion engines.

The electric power train is superior to the piston engine, and this is why the modern EV will win in totally displacing the old style piston engines within the decade of the 2020s.

Will the oil companies face the same fate as Kodak, and resist fundamental change taking them and all their share holders over the cliff? Perhaps. Unless, as energy companies they use their market position and get in front of the clean energy wave and participate.

Either way, the 21st century world cannot be expected to prosper if energy lives in an 18th century paradigm. If the fossil fuel companies don't get "in front" of the renewable energy revolution, they'll perish by it just as Kodak and Polaroid demonstrated before them.

Chapter Eight - Industrial Revolution in the 21st Century

"Saving our planet, lifting people out of poverty advancing economic growth... These are one and the same fight. We must connect the dots between climate change, water scarcity, energy shortages, global health, found security, and woman's empowerment. Solutions to one problem must be solutions for all."

- Ban Ki-moon -

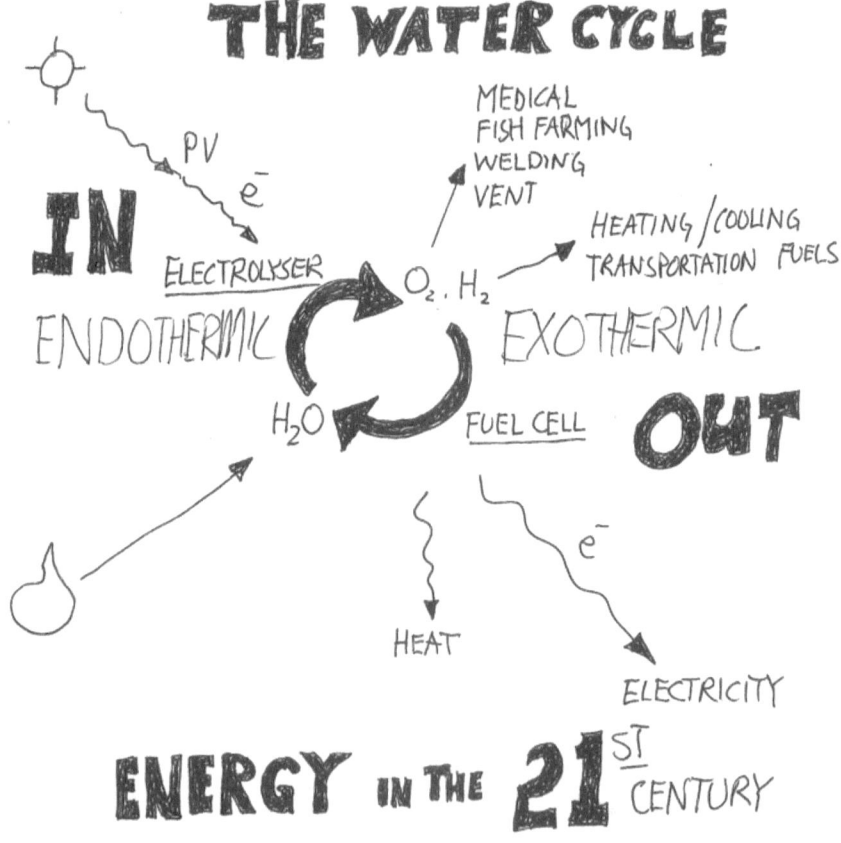

Energy, industrial revolution and social revolution are all intertwined. You can't have one without the others. The evolution of industrial revolution.

History demonstrates over again industrial revolution and social revolution go hand in glove. The industrial revolutions of the 18th, 19th, and 20th centuries all occurred as fuels increased in energy density. The more powerful the fuel, the more powerful the engines innovated to harness this new capability.

The Green New Deal understands the industrial revolution is a continuation of the evolution of industrial revolution by embracing and using the higher energy density of solar fuels.

Just as Coal, and the Steam engine brought us the 18th century, Oil and internal combustion brought us the 19th century. As Natural Gas and Aviation fuels brought us the Jet Age in the 20th century, the industrial revolution of the 21st century is the evolution to solar produced hydrogen, and the Fuel Cell.

Energy, and Engines go hand in hand, just as industrial evolution and human freedoms.

Is it coincidence the American Revolution came on the cusp of the 1st Industrial Revolution? With the enormous expansion of human power amplified by a steam engine came an equally enormous expansion of social and political rights which industrial revolution unleashed and demands.

Is it coincidence the great migration from farms to the cities during the 19th century followed the great migration of jobs from farms to cities to work in factories powered by steam and then diesel engines?

Is it a coincidence, when "energy" was confined to fossil fuels, using exclusive holes in the ground causing extreme inequity among peoples that empire and militarism exploded throughout the 20th century?

Is it a coincidence, so called opponents of a Green New Deal are waving their arms calling such technologies "socialist" in a misguided effort which misses the point entirely. History shows industrial revolution is the greatest impetus for capitalism which ever existed.

Capitalism will flourish in the new economy, the clean energy economy of a Green New Deal, because it empowers individuals. Individuals and small business and large businesses alike. Apply the focus of capitalism to solving problems and problems can be solved, and always as an evolution of industrial revolution.

For an entirely new paradigm of wealth creation, since all humans require energy for almost everything we do, all we need is the right technology, the right gear, and access to solar energy, and water. With only these simple ingredients so to speak, you can power any electrical device, any EV, and home, office or factory anywhere on earth at any scale, or lifestyle. Clean energy based industrial activities expose the big deception of the fossil fuel paradigm: you need to pay them.

Fossil fuels and their restricted control operate as a worldwide mafia. Consider world violence, fossil fuels and the battles to control them, have decimated our history for over three centuries.

Solar energy empowers capitalism by greatly expanding those who can participate.

All people need is a power supply, (a means of production) and the rest is up to them. With energy richness, comes richness in all areas. The reality is the earth is energy rich. We only need to stop burning things out of the ground, and start harvesting the energy falling on our land. The solar power supply already growing our crops, and is the original power supply of our world.

For a brief three hundred years, the world was captured by the quick advantages of harvesting ancient solar energy concentrated into energy dense materials after millions of years of heat and pressure. Fossil fuels are ancient sunlight, concentrated by millions of years of heat and pressure, buried in the ground only to be controlled by a few.

The Green New Deal is about the transition from ancient sunlight, limited by amount available, and high toxicity when used, to the sunlight falling everyday. Fresh sunlight, if you will. Since sunlight is available to people everywhere on earth we don't need to distribute energy to anyone, the energy is already distributed. We only need harvest, store and convert when we want to use it. It's straight forward.

A Green New Deal is the greatest economic opportunity ever seen as trillions of dollars now wasted as fuel costs, and toxic liabilities and impacts can now be redirected into clean energy systems which when paid down only have maintenance costs. No toxicity, and no fuel costs, ever.

Fossil fuels only profit those few who sell them. To choose fossil fuels, toxicity, pollution, economic inequality, militarism, petrodollar supported world terrorism, with high and volatile costs to the consumer only make the case from any objective standpoint fossil fuels offer no solution for a 21st century.

In the 19th century steam engines gave way to internal combustion. In the 21st century Internal combustion engines will give way to the fuel cell and electric drive. A new age of energy is upon us, and it's up to America to take the lead in the transition of the "Hydrocarbon man" into the Silicon man.

The Green New Deal is all about unleashing capitalism to solve real problems at a profit.

As a resource how much is Sunlight worth? At 15 cents per kWh, using 10% conversion into electricity by photovoltaics, about $30/year in electricity per square meter in the Midwest. A square meter is about 10.5 square feet.

If dollar bills were raining down on the parking lot, would you pick some up? The same could be asked about solar energy.

Because electricity has a market value, the solar energy falling on a parking lot, for example, if harvested by solar canopies and converted into usable electricity with solar electric panels (Photovoltaics) used directly to power a load, or dispatched to an electric grid has a real value.

The Solar Energy Resource

Solar energy is measured on earth using Standard Test Conditions (STC). The power rating of solar power at peak sun is described as 1,000 watts per square meter.

Using solar panels we can collect and convert into direct electrical current about 15% of solar Power producing about 150 watts of electrical power, per square meter, at peak.

To calculate the solar Energy available, we multiply the power rating of solar panels by the number of Sun-hour peak equivalent of the solar resource for a given location.

The solar resource depends largely on where you are. To measure the solar energy of any locations we look up the solar resource maps, where these measurements are logged, to find the peak Sun-Hours per day for a given location.

Power multiplied by the Time, equals Energy.

A thousand watts of power (one kW) produced over one Hour produces one kilowatt-hour (kWh) of energy.

The kWh of energy on your electric bill has a cost to the consumer ranging from 7 to 35 cents/kWh depending on your utility and where you live.

In Hawaii, the cost per kWh of electricity is on the high-end around 35 cents/kWh with prices typically lower on the mainland typically ranging from 10 to 28 cents/kWh depending on your utility.

To calculate the Energy harvestable from the solar resource for any place on earth we first define the power rating of the solar panels (Power), and the number of Solar Peak-Hours (Time) measured at the location.

These solar peak hours can be referenced from the Solar Resource Maps for any location. (NREL). The product of Power (kW) multiplied by Time (hours) gives Energy in Kilowatt-hours (kWh).

In Arizona deserts, the solar resource is usually around 6.5 hours per day. In Portland, Oregon due to micro-climate (it rains often) the solar resource is about 3.5 hours per day. In the midwest the Solar peak hour average is about 5.5 hours/day.

The peak hours take the total amount of solar energy striking a surface all day and gives the solar peak-hour equivalent.

To calculate the daily energy production from a solar array, multiply the Power rating of the solar panels by the solar peak hours per day for the location.

Let's answer the question what is solar energy worth?

Example one:

Consider a parking lot with 100 parking stalls. Using average numbers, the area required for a parking space is 300 square feet per parking stall (includes access, driveways, etc.).

Our 100 parking stall parking lot covers, therefore, 30,000 sq. feet. Converting square feet into square meters, the total area is about 2,787 square meters.

If we covered 2,787 square meters with solar panels (on canopies providing shade), for purposes of this example, and use 1,000 watts per square meter (STC conditions) we can capture a solar resource of 2,787,000 watts (optical) at peak.

Over 2.7 Megawatts of solar energy in a given moment before we begin to convert energy into electricity, all from sunlight falling on a small parking lot.

Converting solar power into solar electricity (Photovoltaics) at about 15% gives an electrical power available from our solar panels at 418,050 watts, which is just over 418 kW of electrical power.

To calculate energy, we need to call out a location, perhaps somewhere in the midwest where the average solar resource is 5.5 solar peak hours per day.

To calculate the energy production of our solar array we multiply power (418 kW) by solar peak-hours/day (5.5 hours/day in the midwest) and the electrical energy produced by our parking lot is 2,299 kWh per day.

How much is this worth?

In the midwest it depends on whether you're an industrial, commercial, or residential customer, however, an average cost for electricity is around 15 cents per kWh.

Therefore, we know the value of the solar energy falling on our parking lot at 15 cents/kWh multiplied by 2,229 kWh/day electrical production.

The daily value of solar energy falling on our 100 stall parking lot is worth approximately $334 per day.

Using 30 days per month the value of solar energy falling on our parking lot in the midwest is approximately $10,000 per month in real money.

Ten thousand dollars per month is $120,000 per year as gross income. From an average 100 stall parking lot in the Midwest of America.

Next, what does it cost?

The cost of hardware depends on how you buy it. Just as someone buying a new car has purchase options, the purchaser can buy the system outright, or make a payment plan through equipment lease financing.

To finish our example, 418 kW of solar PV at $0.9/watt system price costs $376,200. An equipment lease package over a 60 month term using Lease Rate Factor 0.025 gives us a monthly payment of $9,600 per month.

The package is profitable to the Lessee the first month producing more income than cost. After 5 years, the equipment is paid down, the lease payments are restructured for the next five years at only maintenance costs which are minimal and a small fraction of the original monthly payment. The profit goes from hundreds per month to thousands per month. The entire power plant is paid down, and still produces energy to be exported to the grid, or used directly with a cost of energy of pennies per kWh, but a market value of 15 cents/kWh.

This is the power economics of solar.

Most people are used to leasing hardware (such as cars) to finance the equipment purchase, or access over the lease term.

If leased, the consumer only pays a monthly payment and is spared coming up with the entire amount for the hardware up-front. Leasing for cars and trucks, and solar energy systems all follow the same structure.

The underwriter of the equipment lease is happy because the monthly payments earn interest, and lucrative producing healthy annual returns. Also, the underwriter holds title of the hardware (asset) until the end of the lease term. At the end of the term the Underwriter can sell, keep, or transfer the asset to the Lessee.

The lease package is self-collateralized as the title to the asset secures the note.

Equipment Lease financing is a way to structure the financial package with qualified hardware at minimal risk (the Underwriter knows the performance of the hardware being financed, and knows the maintenance schedule required to keep the performance over the lease term), as well as title to the hardware securing the package as a collateralized note.

The asset is owned by the Underwriter securing the note until the end of the lease where usually the Lessee chooses to walk away from the hardware, or pay a residual to acquired the fully depreciated asset.

Note: The underwriter defines the financial and performance terms, and length of time under the lease package.

The monthly payment for a 60 month lease, earning the Underwriter 10% annual return (50% over 5 years), can be calculated by multiplying the Capital Expense (cost of the hardware) by a Lease Rate Factor.

In the case of 5 years (the Lessee paying monthly payments for 60 months) a lease rate factor of 0.025 can be applied.

To calculate a Monthly Lease Payment for a given lease, for a 60 month payment schedule multiply the Capital Expense of the hardware ($) by the Lease Rate Factor.

The parking lot owner in our example, could lease a solar energy system and only pay a monthly fee.

Since the value of the solar income is over $10,000, any monthly payment structured lower than $10,000 produces a profit for the owner day one.

From the first payment, the parking lot owner makes profit harvesting a resource formally just wasted making the parking lot hot in the sun, wet in the rain, and slippery in the winter, when it could be shaded by the solar canopies offering multiple benefits in addition to additional monthly profit.

Equipment lease financing, (done everyday when people lease new cars) can be applied to solar energy and renewable energy systems which when amortized into monthly payments can be structured to generate profit for all parties (Lessee and Lessor) starting from the beginning of the lease term package.

This is how the Green New Deal will unleash an entirely new "gold rush" only it won't be gold in the ground, it will be "gold" falling on our parking lots, our building tops and other surfaces which can offer a dual use and generate income.

Chapter Nine - Why the Green New Deal is Good for America

"... We do these things not because they are easy, but because they are hard."

- John F. Kennedy - 1961

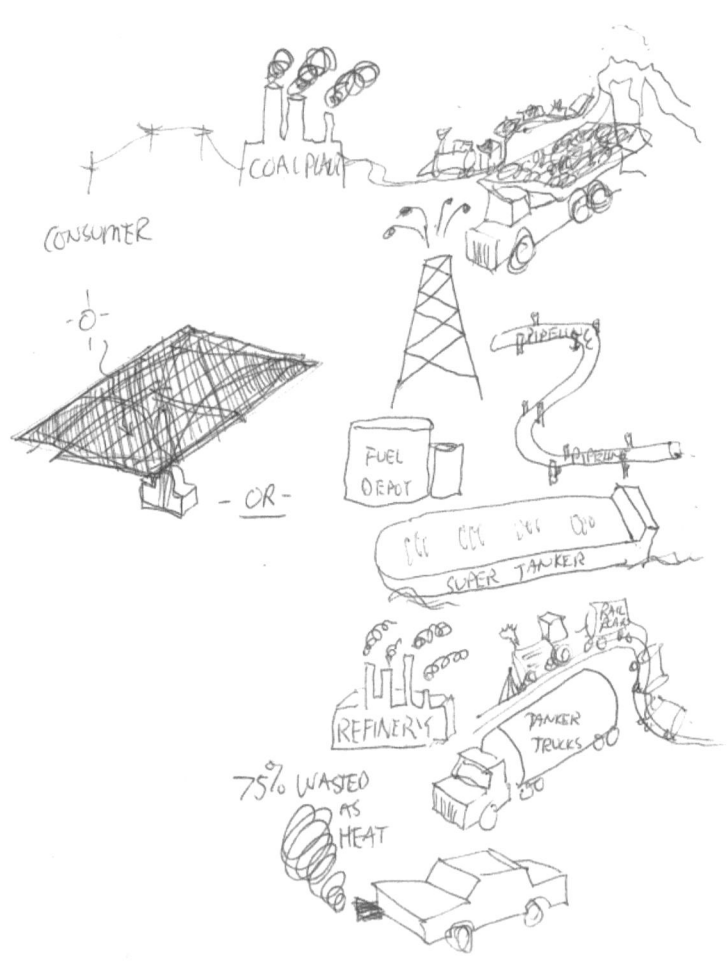

America was forged on the frontier, and to find our spirit again we must reach for the frontier again. Our world is in trouble, and it's in our spirit to respond and lead.

The Green New Deal if good for America because it unleashes the best of what our America constitution seeks to protect: freedom, human dignity, equal opportunity, and prosperity for all her citizens by tapping into a local power supply for electricity and clean transportation fuels.

The Green New Deal transitions the toxic paradigm of centralized fossil fuels, the modern heart of income disparity worldwide causing global disruption on many fronts, into a distributed Carbon-free paradigm of human industrialization with no fuel costs or toxicity threatening present and future generations.

In short, the objective is a sustainable industrial society for the 21st century.

An energy paradigm which promotes human freedom and dignity by providing a power supply distributed among nations as to power all human beings no matter their geographic boundaries or specific location.

The Green New Deal is good for America because clean energy based on Solar electricity and solar clean fuels is better for consumers and our global environment than fossil fuels on all metrics. Solar electricity and clean fuels are more powerful than fossil fuels, therefore we won't need to "live in caves" as so popularly claimed by the fossil fuel interests. Solar Hydrogen being non-toxic allows unlimited use with no deleterious effects on future generations. Being energy rich people can live anyway they choose. This is the heart of freedom.

Solar electricity, and solar produced hydrogen fuel is a universally available energy system from water and sunlight, and returned to water when used thus ultimately resilient and sustainable.

Solar hydrogen offers increased safety, by the nature of hydrogen fuel, with no deaths reported for decades in the industry, as opposed to thousands of people killed each year by burning to death or gravely injured by liquid fossil fuels such as gasoline.

The Green New Deal is good for America because it will lower real levels of toxins and industrial poisons in American soil, biology, air and water. And, inspire the rest of the world in following our lead for a sustainable future.

For America to be safe from toxins, we must inspire all countries to go non-toxic, because through wind and wave, pollution anywhere becomes pollution everywhere.

The Green New Deal is good for America as it defines a new direction in clean energy Infrastructure starting in the Transportation, Residential, Commercial, and Electric Utility sectors by applying clean energy power supplies as a profitable path to systematically replace fossil fuels with clean energy and electric drive.

Increasing solar powered mass transit and the new generation of ride share companies offering access to every type of vehicle from EV cars, and trucks, to the rise of personal mobility devices (PMD) including eScooters, eBikes, eMopeds, eMotorcycles and of course eCars, eTrucks, and soon eRVs will all play a role.

The Green New Deal is good for America as it expands Infrastructure to all Residential, Commercial, and Industrial structures by comprehensively assessing efficiency issues, and the integration of clean energy power systems to lower real costs and limit toxicity onsite.

The Green New Deal is good for America by applying the Government's power of the purse to convert Government buildings, schools, structures, and offices to divert their electric bill from existing fossil fuel sources to renewable energy sources freezing their current energy bills and lowering those bills systematically over a decade to a minimal level around 80% less than currently paid by Government saving billions of dollars in aggregate.

Clean energy lowers the real cost of Government, therefore lowers the tax burden of tax payers, while stimulating industry with huge buying power. Without using any other tools such as taxes, incentives, or rebates a free-market solution exists if only the government would use clean energy towards its own massive energy bill. The power of the purse can include what the government buys everyday as a matter of keeping the doors open.

The Green New Deal is good for America because it organizes Infrastructure projects including basic existing services such as roads and highways, to include installation and application of clean energy powered advanced transportation technologies such as high speed rail, and other conveyances and innovations, which are more efficient and effective than conventional trains, buses, and cars in use over the last 150 years.

Would you rather use an 1850s telegraph to communicate, or a modern smart phone?

In this century, most people would choose the smart phone.

The same is true for Energy, do we stay with steam engines (nuclear power after all is just a dangerous high tech steam engine) of the 18th century, or do we abandon all of this toxic nonsense, and use a 21st century technology which only has four essential parts: solar panels, electrolysers, storage tanks, and fuel cells to power any machine we use today.

The Green New Deal is good for America because it inspires younger Americans that our responsibility, and opportunity is to help each other, and to create a better common future through our example. It demonstrates to younger generations, who must ultimately deal with all our pollution compounded in the future, there is a better way, and a future worth living for. A future worth building.

The Green New Deal is Good for America because it defines and pursues clean energy infrastructure offering able bodied capable Americans, public works projects which provides anyone of qualification and appropriate skill sets to be hired by the contractors involved with the public works.

This is not a guaranteed job, it's a guarantee of the opportunity for work because the government is building public works and the contractors and vendors need people to work.

Jobs for able bodied qualified Americans seeking work, paying taxes, building clean energy infrastructure is a real path forward.

America's physical infrastructure is currently in great disrepair.

A transition to infrastructure equipped with solar energy capture, storage and dispatch systems opens new options for travel, powering and heating homes, commercial buildings and industrial loads. A new power supply.

An energy industry which offers more energy at lower cost for all sectors of manufacturing, transportation, heating and cooling, and powering all our electronic devices and conveyances.

The Green New Deal is good for America because it returns to our roots. Principles of innovation, self-reliance, self-determination, hard work, benefits not only for ourselves, our families, and all Americans which share this great country, but for all people who share this earth. It's in our American interests to see a growing stable world.

The Green New Deal is good for America because it taps into the American spirit to solve seemly unsolvable problems by applying our technology, and our will to do the right thing for future generations and respond to our grand responsibility.

Beyond all other countries as our constitution defends individual rights, America is best suited to this task, after all, tackling frontiers is in our American fiber. America was born on the frontier, grew up on the frontier, and now can solve all of the major problems facing our world: by leading the transition from toxic Carbon to non-toxic Carbon free solar fuels.

The Industrial Revolution of the 21st century is a natural evolution of industrial revolution: the Green New Deal and the path towards a mutually prosperous and peaceful world. An advanced civilization of the 21st century.

Chapter Ten - The New Economy

"If we had a hydrogen economy worldwide, every nation on earth would create its own energy source to support its economy, and the threat of war over diminishing resources would just evaporate."

- Dennis Weaver -

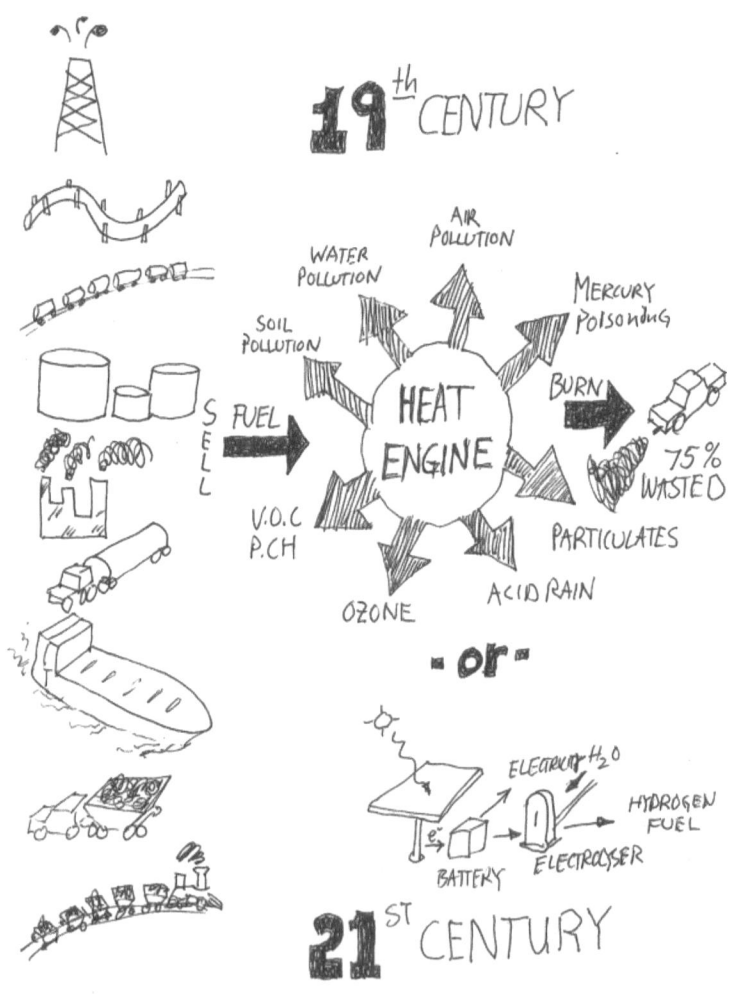

The New Economy emerging from the Green New Deal sets America on a path of detoxing our world, and unleashing human enterprise.

Leadership in the global community of nations towards expanding individual dignity, human rights, and the freedoms clean energy empowers to energy consumers across all sectors, and markets local and global.

The New Economy embraces the transition of the old "Hydrocarbon Man" into the "Silicon Man." The transition from commodity to self-sufficiency.

The 21st century has technology in its grasp undreamed by all generations daring not to conceive of a world emerging with dignity for all, and the opportunity freedom and entrepreneurship offers its citizens in their pursuit of happiness, and sustained economic prosperity.

In the 21st century human poverty is totally unnecessary, and can be solved as simply as applying solar powered UV water sterilizers. Just as vaccines have saved millions, so can applying solar energy technology on the most direct needs: clean water.

Technology Leaps

We've seen the enormous growth of digital technology in the telephone business transforming modern civilization in only a few decades from hard wires to wireless touching every corner of the world. Where a landline was impossible, the wireless finds easy and no trouble in comparison. That's how the world changes. Step, step, leap.

For over a century to use the telephone required a physical "wire" in between the parties no matter the distance between them. An entire network of landlines were built around the world over a century of building and connecting almost every large community on earth. An investment of trillions of dollars.

Within one decade the "wireless" phone had completely transformed the communications industry - such an event unimaginable for over a century. In one decade, the entire worldwide telephone business was changed at its roots. The world evolved from "wired up" to "wireless." This is an example of disruptive technology, and how a leap in technology leaves the old ways behind opening up bold new frontiers of communications, manufacturing and transportation.

In this same way a Green New Deal will be disruptive to old inefficient toxic industries, winning over their markets with innovation, efficiency, and non toxicity - real value for the customer. This is the natural way of things. The new which is better, replaces the old which is not.

When the "new" offers so many benefits over the old way of doing things, natural market forces cannot contain it.

Despite the objections of the old industry early on, such as writing off "wireless" as "Government control of industry," or any number of falsehoods eerily similar to the opposition now voiced by those who do not understand the Green New Deal, the advantages of innovation just simply outweigh the costs of the old technology.

As happened with Kodak, or Polaroid when the digital camera came to market. Two companies over a century old founded in the 1800s, destroyed within a decade.

All because they didn't understand the impact of disruptive technology on their business. Before the digital camera, everyone used film which needed developing (great aftermarket income). After the digital camera came to market, almost no one needed film developed. So abrupt was the transition, Kodak and Polaroid completely missed it. After dominating their industry from the 1800s, they no longer exist.

The fossil fuel companies should take note.

The industrial revolution in communications from hard wire to wireless is a fact. At first the old industries couldn't understand the situation they faced. Those who adapted to the new technology thrived, and made even more money. Those who ignored, or tried to ignore the new reality failed and disappeared. Fossil fuel companies and countries funded by petrodollars are acting like Kodak and Polaroid before them. Literally, their heads in the sand.

The industrial revolution of energy moving away from commodity based Carbon fuels, requiring moving materials all over the world, and into a Carbon-free, no fuel-cost paradigm unleashes new wealth for all economies everywhere on earth because it empowers individuals on location.

Unleashing a commercial and economic renaissance which eliminates the inherent income disparity of a fossil fuel world requiring reoccurring payments for fuels delivered, launches a world of self sufficiency for all people, raising their individual freedom, dignity and economic prosperity.

Just as "wireless" technology transformed the communications industry, so will "wireless" grid independent energy systems obsolete the century old business models of utility and energy companies based on centralized fossil fuels.

The new energy paradigm, as a natural evolution, will obsolete the outdated notion of Carbon based fuels burned by our ancestors. Instead of being based in the ground, the new economy and energy paradigm will be based in the sky. Sunlight and water is all the 21st century needs. Whoever leads in this transition will benefit most, and, intrinsic to this technology whoever uses it wins. Why?

Toxicity, and energy costs go down in real time for the consumer. Energy users can tap into primary power without any middlemen, all they need is the right equipment. The greatest economic stimulus we can provide an economy is increased reliability and resilience of energy supply at lower cost.

Also, we take on and solve 17 global toxic catastrophes in the balance.

A solar hydrogen economy is the only energy paradigm which can achieve this goal.

The New Economy, based on traditional American values of Freedom, Independence, and Prosperity can reach not just the few as it is with fossil fuel providers, but to all who wish to tap into the power supply which has been powering human life and life on earth since time began: the sun.

The sun powers the natural world. It can also power the industrial, and provide growth for centuries to come. No other energy paradigm can offer this unbridled opportunity to grow without the destruction of the environment which would certainly otherwise occur with continued use of toxic fossil fuels.

The New Economy based on a Green New Deal is based on the creation of wealth powered by the sun. It's available, powerful, and able to power human industrial activity to levels much higher and unattainable by fossil fuels. The new economy based on Solar Hydrogen offers more power, and more freedom - not less.

The solar hydrogen economy offers electricity, and clean fuels on demand by converting abundant natural renewable energy into storage for dispatch in industrial quantities when desired.

Isn't that the whole point, after all? Energy on demand with no fuel costs, or pollution.

No fracking, no drilling, no strip mining, no deep mining. No supertankers, no railroads of coal and oil, no refineries or fuel depots. No toxicity, no Green house gasses, no NOx, SOx, Mercury, radiation, particulates, or any of the other toxins including but not limited to volatile organic compounds (VOC), partially consumed hydrocarbons (PCH), and other serious toxins - all resulting from burning Carbon.

The answer to the world's toxicity problem is simple: stop burning Carbon. Replace Carbon fuels with solar produced hydrogen from water. Solar hydrogen systems can provide any level of industrial capacity desired being entirely scalable from small loads, through transportation, residential, commercial, and industrial loads.

Freedom is the key to prosperity. The Green New Deal is all about creating new wealth, where solar resources were left before to overheat parking lots and the tops of buildings needing to be cooled, the new economy harvests that energy formerly wasted and turns it into hard currency: electricity for use, onsite, and for the benefit of the consumer.

The Green New Deal is not about the Government control of industries, often touted by opposition in a ploy to induce fear and confusion in their constituents, and indeed just another campaign of disinformation.

The objective is not for Government to control industries, but to act in the common defense, and in favor of the common welfare to use the power of the purse to not further fossil fuels and the destruction of the natural world through accumulating toxicity.

Rather, transition to a sustainable more powerful future expanding access and application of industrial strength energy without the pitfalls of toxicity and fuel costs which are causing such global disruption.

The new economy responds to markets created when we solve problems. We have many problems to solve as America leads the global effort to transition into a sustainable industrial society. A growth industry will be the process of cleaning up the enormous amounts of pollution accumulated in our soils, air, waterways and biology. There is much work to do to begin mitigating our toxic footprint.

Plastics in the Oceans

A Green New Deal recognizes the mounting catastrophe of plastic waste and debris in the oceans and other water bodies. Plastics are mostly made from Petroleum, using formulas which cause the plastic to not degrade for centuries. Designing plastics for single use which last centuries is another insanity of a fossil fuel world.

Plastics break up, but they don't break down. One piece of plastic garbage in the ocean, breaks into two pieces, then four, then eight, sixteen, you see the trend.

The problem with petroleum based plastics as they break up into smaller and smaller pieces is they become more easily consumed by wildlife and fish.

It's accumulative. Algae and small fish absorb and consume micro plastics. Bigger fish eat the smaller fish, with the largest fish in the seas eating those contaminated bait fish with humans eating the large fish and the toxins in their flesh. The plastics, and the toxins accumulate chemically polluting the entire fisheries from the smallest creature to the largest.

We're chocking the oceans with billions of pieces of plastic becoming trillions and beyond. This is another example of a global crisis which needs immediate attention and someone needs to lead. America can lead. The Green New Deal is a concerted effort to get to the root of the problem, and fix it.

America can lead in using bioplastics and other formulations and feedstocks which are formulated to have a rapid breakdown.

We can engineer plastics to be biodegradable. If America leads this industry we can transform billion dollar industries into profitable and sustainable ones, without sacrificing all the fish in the seas and future generations. We achieve this though the leadership of our example for the rest of the world to follow.

We can develop and apply new technology to begin retrieving the plastics spread all over the earth for recycling or decomposition.

This requires new technology, and creates new jobs. Most of all, it requires we unleash the creative power of American capitalism and have the government influence to help, not retard these efforts.

America needs to be on the side of right. America needs to be on the side of future generations. If we're true to our grandchildren's interests, we're being true Americans.

The Green New Deal does not seek to redistribute wealth. The Green New Deal is about creating new wealth.

The clean energy economy is all about solving problems, and doing so at a profit. Our global civilization is under threat by the very weight of our energy dependence as energy has been dominated by carbon and its control. Totally, unnecessary.

If we grow burning carbon, we need to burn more carbon to keep growing. This is going be replaced with a new economy which is carbon free.

If energy is carbon free, then it's non-toxic. This is our greatest responsibility to future generations: a reduced level of toxicity, not increased toxicity, as a fossil fuel world would surely be.

The Solar Resource - Distributed Energy

It takes a lot of energy to power our modern world. It takes more than we have, if we continue a fossil fuel world.

There isn't enough fossil fuel to raise 7 billion people above the poverty level, let alone modern lifestyles.

Further, burning that much Carbon would collapse the biology of earth long before you reached 7 billion people all living with a North American modern life style (250 kWh/person/day). Clearly, a better energy paradigm is required.

The solar resource is the only power supply which can provide enough energy distributed to all people with enough power density and energy density per day to provide the Gigawatt-hours of energy daily required by the people of earth in the modern age.

Using solar electricity to produced totally non-toxic and high power hydrogen fuel for our heavy machinery provides a massive step forward in the evolution of human civilization from fossil fuels to the solar hydrogen economy.

The Green New Deal is the evolution of industrial revolution. The revolution for industrial sustainability, and the future of our modern civilization.

Chapter Eleven - Epilogue

"... we set sail on this new sea, because there is new knowledge to be gained, and new rights to be won. And they must be won, and used on the progress of all people..."

- John F. Kennedy - 1961

As Americans we hold a sacred trust. To value, protect and personify our greatest accomplishment - our American Constitution. The laws that bind us.

Americans have many outward faces, but we are one people under our Constitution, one people under the skin. We are one people, because we are all people.

Our American constitution is what truly separates us from the world.

American exceptionalism isn't based on bluster, it's based on the frontier spirit. It's based on the exceptionalism of our constitution and how we live it, and our responsibility to ourselves, each other, and future generations.

How we live as a constitutional republic makes us uniquely, and distinctly American. For over 240 years we've individually and collectively fought for the dignity of the human experience. It's been a hard road, but we live everyday with the fruits from the sacrifices of our fathers and mothers, and forefathers to keep the light of our constitution alive as we grow through the centuries.

Our constitution defines and defends an individual's right of dignity, freedom, justice under the law, and happiness in the pursuit of happiness.

Implicit in our individual and therefore collective rights are the rights and expectations of clean air, clean water, clean soils, forests, deserts, waterways, biological diversity, clean food and the integrity of DNA, and all other natural resources we've been endowed with, and are responsible. The right to be different, unique and absolutely our own in self-determination is the legacy of our constitution, and our quality of life depends on being faithful to the values and purpose of our constitution as outlined so eloquently in our preamble.

The preamble of the Constitution brings us together in common starting "we the people." The responsibility and honor of our government is described in our preamble and includes our collective responsibilities including "promote the general welfare."

A Green New Deal lives in the spirit of our preamble, and thrives in the creative and economic explosion of new wealth a Green New Deal would bring not only to ourselves as Americans, but to all other nations. A sustainable industrial future. A future which can only happen if we have an answer to global toxicity and climate disruption.

Climate Disruption from human activities burning Carbon fuels is a call for "Provide for the common defense." The pentagon has already stated that climate change is our greatest foe presenting the greatest danger to our country. We must respond if future generations will have any quality of life known to this generation.

America can bring to the world a solution which is universal enabling all people anywhere on earth the physical means to participate in the 21st century with advanced technology, powered with clean energy at their will.

Solar based energy enables diverse cultures to maintain their heritage and identity by keeping their way of life. This is what we owe each other. Individual freedom, is the foundation upon which global freedom will ring. Addressing global toxicity is a task we must take to heart if freedom is to truly grow in the 21st century. Without health, there can't be life. True for a human being, and an entire world. For true freedom we need to start cleaning up our industrial path. Our collective global health.

The Green New Deal is the power supply, literally, for this freedom. If you can make you're own energy, you truly have freedom. Industrial based freedom.

Any village anywhere on earth can live as they wish, just as any city. When they need water sterilized, just flip on the solar powered UV water sterilizer, and their kids won't die of water borne diseases. It's really that simple. If, you have the right gear.

There's no need to drill, frack, strip, or mine anything to have access to energy. Solar energy technology is all you need to power the device to sterilize water. Need more clean water? Use a bigger machine. It's really that straight forward. If you have the right technology, you're good to go. If you don't, you haven't a chance.

A Green New Deal is all about enabling a universal power supply, the sun, to power people with 21st century energy demands. A power supply with universal access, low costs, an no toxicity to harm present, or future generations. The world can be energy rich and modern in lifestyle should people wish to live that way. And the implications for human society all over the world has never seen such a leap in empowerment.

Poverty is a human institution. There are no laws of physics which requires anyone to be impoverished. A solar powered world is an energy rich world accessible by anyone.

Under any fossil fuel scenario, poverty will always exist. It's just not economically viable to transport and sell Carbon fuels to everyone on earth in the any quantity near what's required to bring everyone above the poverty level. The solution? Use energy already distributed. Hence, the sun.

A Green New Deal is a 21st century revolution bringing everyone out of the dark ages of fossil fuel based energy.

The billion plus people without reliable electricity, or electricity access at all, can all be brought into the 21st century in one decade.

America, should be the leader of this industrial, economic and social revolution. Much as we've always been on the forefront of technological revolution and the social improvements which manifest.

The world is facing a crisis. A crisis of 18th century energy technology trying to do a 21st century job. It is in light of this crisis of toxicity, this crisis of excessive and volatile energy costs leaving entire countries without reliable power, from which a new energy paradigm will rise.

This new energy economy is the basis of a Green New Deal.

Our global modern civilization faces 17 environmental catastrophes anyone of which would be a crisis on its own. Seventeen major crises all at once ensures our eventual collapse unless we change the one thing linking all of these crises: burning carbon.

Isn't it amazing? Such diverse crises including ocean acidification, green house gases (CO_2), partially consumed hydrocarbons (PCH), volatile organic compounds (VOC), endocrine disruptors, NOx, SOx, Mercury poisoning, particulates, ozone, radiation, heavy metals, acid rain, species loss, plastic waste from petroleum, DNA degradation, and

Climate Disruption can all be solved doing one thing: stop burning carbon.

NASA used fuel cells on Apollo for good reasons. High power, some heat (useful in space), and when the fuel (hydrogen) and oxidant (oxygen) are used the only waste product is pure water (also useful for the astronauts). NASA used Fuel Cells because it was the best technology for the job. The same is true now, 50 years later for our world.

On plant earth we are the astronauts, and the same energy requirements apply to us. If piston engines are insufficient for spacecraft, why not apply the same standards for our industry. NASA chose fuel cells. So should we.

The greatest economic revolution is taking hold where the old toxic fossil fuel, pay as you go model goes obsolete replaced by a solar powered non-toxic high power technology with no fuel costs.

The profitable use of solar energy onsite to power industrial loads including individual needs, homes, commercial buildings, industrial factories, as well as the electrification of transportation will transform the 21st century expanding markets and easing international tensions by providing energy self-sufficiency for all countries.

A stable prosperous earth is the objective. The only way to tap into the vast amount of energy required for the modern lifestyle of human civilization depends on energy capable of fueling our growth now, and into future decades.

Thermodynamically, there is no other power supply capable of providing so much energy to so many people in so many locations. There is only one way it can be done in sufficient quantities daily, if we want to obsolete global poverty: the sun.

The sun powers the natural world. The sun can now power our industrial world and a new era of industrial revolution is embarked upon as we understand we need to solve 17 major problems at once.

Our only path to achieving this is the clean energy revolution recognized by the Green New Deal and the fundamental relationships between our global toxic crisis, and global liberation from the chains of fossil fuels.

All Americans have the right to clean air, clean soil, clean water, clean food, and clean DNA for a healthy future. Rights we share in common with everyone else. Perhaps that's the one thing that truly makes us human - our shared humanity.

Humanity towards ourselves, each other, and this earth we share with all life. Our humanity is in our stewardship of the human ethic, the quality of life for each individual. The dignity of human civilization at its best.

The Green New Deal embraces this responsibility and works to forge a truly sustainable, prosperous, and inclusive economy worldwide delivering real growth for all people for centuries to come based on human dignity, self-reliance, self-determination and industrial sustainability for everyone on earth.

www.ingramcontent.com/pod-product-compliance
Lightning Source LLC
Chambersburg PA
CBHW061314280526
45784CB00002B/980